Hikernut's

Grand Canyon Companion

A Guide to Hiking
the Most Popular Trails into the Canyon

Bright Angel,
South Kaibab &
North Kaibab Trails

Brian J. Lane

Edited by Kathleen Bryant
Art Direction by Larry Lindahl
Text, photographs, maps, and graphics
by Brian J. Lane
With additional thanks to Pamela & John Chionis

NOTE: The author assumes no liability for any injury or damages resulting from the use of information contained herein. The maps provided in this guide are for illustrative purposes only. They are not to scale and are not intended for use in route finding. Each has been hand drawn, and if you don't see inconsistencies between each map, you're not looking hard enough. A detailed topographic map of the area is necessary before hiking and backpacking.

FIRST EDITION

ISBN-13: 978-0-9790230-0-2
ISBN-10: 0-9790230-0-9
Library of Congress Control Number: 2006910176

Published by: A Sense of Nature
2940 Red Rock Loop Road
Sedona, AZ 86336

Many of the photographs included in this book are available at:
www.aSenseofNature.com
or e-mail: hikernut@commspeed.net

Background photo: Bright Angel Creek looking toward the South Rim
from the bridge at Bright Angel Campground.

Cover photo: John Chionis at Coconino Overlook—the beginning of our journey
from the North Rim to the South Rim of the canyon.

About the Author

Born and raised in North Brookfield, Massachusetts, I've lived in Arizona since 1992. My wife La Quita and I have a small ranch near Sedona where we raise our animals and grow veggies. A former U.S. Marine, I've attended Clark University, Massachusetts College of Art, and Kaplan University, majoring in art, media, and paralegal studies, among others. I am also a horticulturist, forestry and wildlife conservationist, and master watershed steward advocating for watershed ecosystems and sustainable resource management.

As for the "Hiker nut" moniker...I've been using it since the first time I signed up for an email account some years ago. I figured that giving myself such an address would help ensure that I continued to get out there and keep hiking. The nickname also came about due to the so called "crazy" pace I tend to keep when hiking uphill.

La Quita says that some people are called to the canyon, and I guess I'm one. The canyon is an odd dichotomy of beauty and harshness. In the early

Brian at Bright Angel Trailhead after hiking out from Phantom Ranch.

morning climbing out, panting and puffing, all I have to do is look at the sunlight slowly pouring into the canyon and I can't help but smile. I hike the canyon to experience its incomparable scenery, for the challenge of hiking such a rugged area, and as a test of my fitness. Hiking the canyon forces me to get out there, stay fit, and physically push myself. I believe those who don't test themselves—exerting oneself past the point of physical discomfort—will never really know themselves.

Hike smart and have fun!

Brian Lane
Sedona, Arizona

This book is dedicated to my dearest hiking and life companion, my wife La Quita, for all her patience, input, and support. Further dedication goes out to Mom, Dad, Sue, Rob, & the rest of our family; we love you. Thanks too for all my other backcountry hiking partners, John Ducasse, Mike Hubacz, David Woods, Glenn Southworth, Ron Chambers, Tamara Snyder and family, Alvin Derouen, John and Jim Chionis, and Larry Lindahl.

Photo: Yavapai Point sunset, South Rim.

Table of Contents

Afoot and light-hearted, I take to the open trail,
Healthy, free, the world before me, The long brown path before me, leading wherever I choose.

Henceforth I ask not good fortune—I myself am good fortune;
Henceforth I whimper no more, postpone no more, need nothing, Strong and content,
I travel the canyon trail.

Adapted from the first two stanzas of Walt Whitman's "*Song of the Open Road*"

Photo: South Kaibab Trail approaching the Tonto Trail Junction.

Chapter One

Introduction

There is this to be
said for walking:
It's the one mode of
human locomotion
by which a man
proceeds on his own
two feet, upright,
erect, as a man
should be, not
squatting on his
rear haunches
like a frog.

Edward Abbey

S o, you want to hike into the Grand Canyon. I don't blame you. It is one of the most spectacular natural wonders in the world, and the only way to really see it in all its splendor is by going below the rim. On a partly cloudy day as the clouds cause shadows to undulate in, out, and around the multi-colored rock formations, it is incomparable in its beauty. To venture and explore the inner canyon is to gain a fresh perspective that very few of the nearly five million visitors each year ever dare to undertake.

I have written this guide as an introduction, mainly for novices, to the most popular trails of the inner canyon, commonly called the Central Corridor Trails: Bright Angel, South Kaibab, and North Kaibab Trails. These are the easily followed, well-maintained trails. There are usually plenty of other folks on the trail to assist you if you find yourself in a predicament. All other trails into the Grand Canyon are considered wilderness trails. They are not maintained, require advanced route-finding skills, and are not advised for first-time canyon travelers.

A view of the Inner Canyon looking down at the confluence of Bright Angel Creek and the Colorado River from South Kaibab Trail.

If you have never hiked or backpacked into the canyon, this condensed book has been designed so it could be taken with you during the trip. It includes trail descriptions, trip planning information, some helpful hints, rudimentary maps, and contact information.

As for my own personal background, I have been hiking and backpacking in the canyon for over a decade now, and have traveled most inner canyon trails during nearly 30 overnight trips. I have had my day pack opened and riffled through by a raven, fallen on the trail more than once, and suffered through a bout of stomach virus that kept me up all night prior to one hike out. Add to that some of my other backpacking experiences in the High Sierras, San Juan Mountains, and Alaska (to name a few favorites), and I figure I have enough experience to issue a little practical advice, providing the reader and potential canyon traveler with a few of my perceptions

 Side Step: Canyon Facts

The Grand Canyon is over 5,000 vertical feet deep, 18 miles wide, 277 river miles long, and the North Rim is nearly 1,200 feet higher in elevation than the South Rim. While the South Rim receives about 5 million visitors each year, the North Rim sees only about one-tenth that amount of visitation. This is primarily due to easier highway access to the South Rim, the greater amount of canyon views and services available on the South Rim, and the fact that the North Rim is officially closed from mid-October through mid-May.

It wasn't until the year 1540 that the first white folks even set eyes on the canyon, at which time they seemed to disregard its beauty and deemed it more of an impediment to their travels than one of the most majestic natural wonders on Earth. They also believed the Colorado River, as seen from the South Rim, was about six feet wide, when the average width is actually 300 feet across. In and around the canyon there are approximately 75 different mammal species, 50 reptile species, 25 fish species, and 300 species of birds. It is a truly unique environment.

on how to manage it all. I hope you'll find most of this information useful, and hope even more that you enjoy your Grand Canyon Central Corridor experience as much as I have always enjoyed my own. The canyon is truly one of the most visually stunning, spectacular, and awe inspiring sights in the world.

Claret cup cactus in bloom.

Beware though. Hiking and backpacking the Grand Canyon is a very different experience from any other hike you've ever done. It will do you good to remember that over 250 people must be rescued from the canyon each year, while the National Park Service reports that it annually responds to approximately 400 medical emergencies throughout the park. It is an inverted mountain, dropping nearly 5,000 vertical feet in less than 8 to 10 miles, descending seemingly endless zigzagged switchbacks on any trail that ventures below the rim. Unlike mountain travel that usually parallels a river or creek, nearly all natural drainages in the canyon are dry. The elevation change is equal to starting in the cool high mountains of Flagstaff, Arizona, and ending up at the canyon's bottom in a climate equivalent to the hot low desert environment of Phoenix. You can expect a minimum temperature change of about 20 degrees from the South Rim to the Colorado River, and you should plan on taking twice as much time to climb out of the canyon as it took you going in.

Most people find hiking the canyon much more difficult than they had imagined. A proper fitness level, positive mental attitude, and a measure of common sense are all required. Those traits—combined with the necessities of adequate water, food, and proper emergency supplies—can keep you alive and help make for a safe and pleasant trip. And still…under the best of conditions you should anticipate emerging from the canyon tired and sore for a few days, and about three to five pounds lighter in body weight. The canyon is a harsh, dangerous, rugged, and very hot environment. Water sources are few and very far between, while the upward and downward stints are relentless. Blistered feet, ankle sprains, and dehydration are common maladies and should be expected unless

4

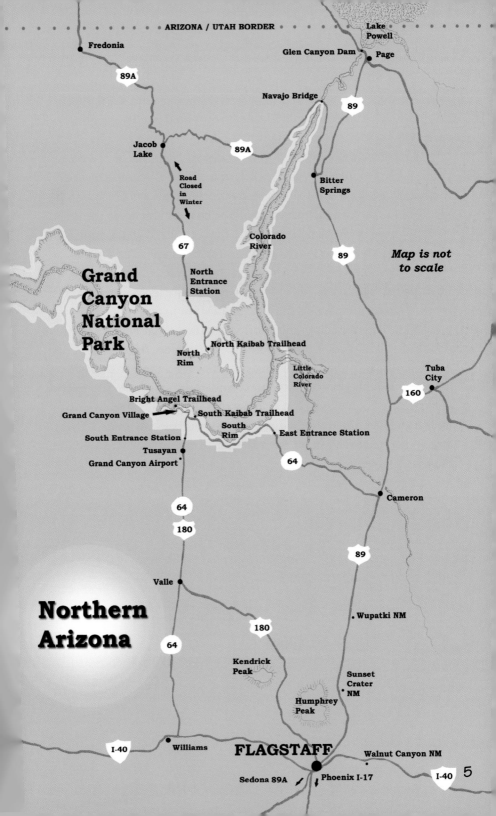

extra care is taken. If, for any reason, you require emergency evacuation while hiking in the Grand Canyon you will be charged the cost of the rescue. Remember that under most circumstances cell phones do not work in the canyon and therefore should not be relied upon for any reason.

All information contained in this book is based on my own particular backpacking experiences and other things I have learned over the years. I do not assume responsibility for any injury or damage resulting from the use of information provided herein. (You know the drill.)

The other disclaimer I must invoke is that nearly all the information provided in this book is subject to change. The system at Grand Canyon National Park concerning permits, shuttles, and general information seems to vary to some degree each season; trails can wash out completely during summer monsoon storms; water pipes can break; medical and nutritional advice can change as new science evolves; and so on. I do hope to provide updates and corrections to this publication as feasible, but each individual desiring to enter the canyon should address any concerns he or she might have with a park ranger by visiting or calling the Grand Canyon Backcountry Office, (see page 84). Remember too that Arizona does not observe Daylight Saving Time and remains on Mountain Standard Time year round.

View of the canyon with fresh snowfall on the South Rim.

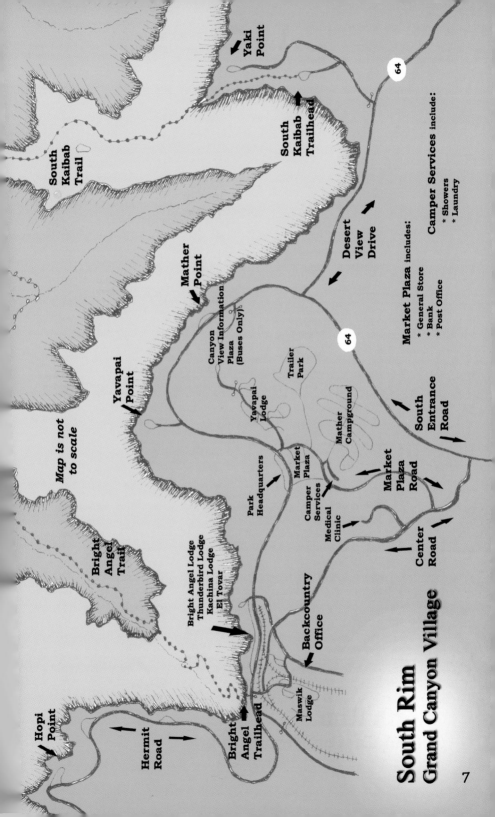

Yaki Point

64

South Kaibab Trail

South Kaibab Trailhead

Desert View Drive

Mather Point

Market Plaza includes:
* General Store
* Bank
* Post Office

Camper Services include:
* Showers
* Laundry

Yavapai Point

Map is not to scale

Canyon View Information Plaza (Buses Only)

64

Trailer Park

Yavapai Lodge

Mather Campground

Market Plaza

South Entrance Road

Park Headquarters

Camper Services

Medical Clinic

Market Plaza Road

Center Road

Bright Angel Trail

Bright Angel Lodge
Thunderbird Lodge
Kachina Lodge
El Tovar

Backcountry Office

Maswik Lodge

Bright Angel Trailhead

Hopi Point

Hermit Road

South Rim
Grand Canyon Village

7

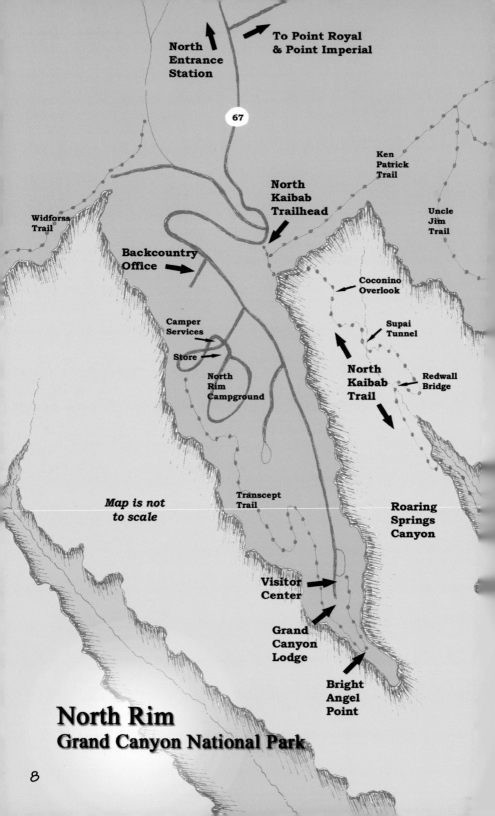

North Entrance Station

To Point Royal & Point Imperial

67

Ken Patrick Trail

Widforss Trail

North Kaibab Trailhead

Uncle Jim Trail

Backcountry Office

Coconino Overlook

Supai Tunnel

Camper Services

Store

North Kaibab Trail

Redwall Bridge

North Rim Campground

Map is not to scale

Transcept Trail

Roaring Springs Canyon

Visitor Center

Grand Canyon Lodge

Bright Angel Point

North Rim
Grand Canyon National Park

Ribbon Falls is located about a mile and a half south of Cottonwood Campground on the North Kaibab Trail.

 ## Side Step: My First Time in the Canyon

OK, picture this: It is a beautiful April morning and I'm about 1.5 miles into my first backpacking trip into the canyon. I have an external frame backpack, and my sleeping bag, wrapped in a slick nylon stuff sack, is very tightly bound by half-inch nylon rope. The mule train comes up in back of the group I'm with, so we step off to the inside of the trail. Just as the mules are passing I decide to adjust my pack. Somehow my over-taut sleeping bag hits a rock jutting out from the trail wall and literally pops into the air, making a graceful arc and landing about six feet away, and underneath one of the mules. Now I'm trying to grab my sleeping bag with my hiking stick, as it begins to roll underneath this mule and possibly over the edge and down the canyon never to be seen again. The mule is pretty wild-eyed as he senses something bouncing around underneath him and the guy riding on the mule begins to freak out with fear as the mule starts to do a little cha-cha on the trail. I am now close enough that I quickly grab the closure string from the stuff sack and snatch my errant sleeping bag from beneath the belly of the dancing mule. After a weak smile and sheepish "sorry," I repack my sleeping bag and check to ensure it will not escape again; the crisis had been averted.

Chapter Two

Permits and Logistics

I may not have
gone where I
intended to go,
but I think I have
ended up where I
intended to be.

Douglas Adams

Mather Point is located along the South Entrance Road on the South Rim of the canyon.

The first thing to remember is this. Unless you really love the heat (temperatures in the shade can reach well over 110 degrees), you should avoid venturing into the canyon in the summer months. I know that thousands do it every year, but the effects of dehydration can easily and severely impair judgment and turn your backcountry adventure into a nightmarish trip to the hospital. I want you to enjoy the canyon, just as I have for years, and since I do not like the heat (I admit that I am a native New Englander, and therefore I'm a bit more comfortable in fog), I have never backpacked between the months of June and August. Nonetheless, hiking the canyon in the summer can be easily accomplished with proper planning. If you must travel during this time of year please remember to hike only during early morning and late afternoon. Carry ample water (at least a quart for every hour of hiking), including sport drinks with electrolytes, and avoid hauling a full pack in the heat of midday at all cost.

Never attempt to go from the rim of the canyon to the Colorado River and back in the same day. To hike round trip from rim to river in a day, especially in the heat of summer, is foolhardy and causes many emergency rescues each year.

If you will be traveling into the canyon during the summer, make sure to plan ahead and see to it that you are not hiking during the hottest part of the day, from about 10 a.m. through 4 p.m. Shuttle bus schedules are adjusted seasonally in order to accommodate very early morning (4 a.m. in July) and evening hikers (an hour after sunset). If you plan on utilizing the park busses, verify these schedules when planning your hike.

South Rim Backcountry Office.

Backcountry Permits

To travel overnight into the canyon you must first obtain a permit from the Backcountry Information Center at Grand Canyon National Park. The permit is required for all overnight use, although it is not required for overnight stays at the cabins or dorms of Phantom Ranch. All contact information for permits and concessionaires is provided near the end of this book (see page 84).

There are basically two ways to apply for a permit. You can apply in person at either Backcountry Information Center. There are Backcountry Offices located at the South Rim and another at the North Rim; they are open daily from 8 a.m. to noon and 1 p.m. to 5 p.m. (although the North Rim is closed from mid-October through mid-May). Your second option is to complete the Backcountry Permit Request Form (see page 86) and fax or mail the request to the Grand Canyon Backcountry Office. The Park Service may offer email permits in the near future.

Advanced permits are highly recommended, especially during the months of highest use, from mid-spring to mid-autumn. Walk-in permits for the Central Corridor during the busy season are very difficult to obtain and should not be counted on.

The earliest date you can apply for a permit is the first day of the month, four months before your proposed starting date. For example, if your start date is in May, you can apply on January 1st. Keep in mind that about 30,000 people apply for backcountry permits each year and less than half that number are issued. To help make sure your application is accepted, apply as soon as possible and provide alternate dates. It can take three to six weeks to process the application. Requests that are received less than three weeks before a start date may be automatically denied. Another option if your permit is declined is to contact the Havasupai Tribe and pack into Havasu Canyon (see page 84). This trail, while not your classic Grand Canyon hike, is less arduous and takes you to a beautiful oasis of blue-green water that includes the most photographed waterfall in Arizona.

There are three campgrounds along the Central Corridor trails (with their National Park Backcountry Key Codes). **Indian Garden Campground (CIG)** sits about halfway between the South Rim and the south side of the Colorado River along Bright Angel Trail. **Bright Angel Campground (CBG)** is located at the bottom of the canyon, adjacent to Phantom Ranch, near the confluence of Bright Angel Creek and the Colorado River. The last of the inner-canyon campgrounds is **Cottonwood Campground (CCG)**, along the North Kaibab Trail about halfway between Phantom Ranch and the North Rim. (See trail reference maps on pages 43, 48, and 54.) From October through April the trail north from Cottonwood Campground is essentially closed to the North Rim. The Park Service issues fewer permits for Cottonwood Campground, which has no water from October through April (unless you filter water

The North Rim Backcountry Office (shown in its current form) may be relocated by 2008.

from Bright Angel Creek running adjacent to the campground). Each campground has drinking water and toilets, except as previously noted above.

At this time, the fee for a permit is $10, plus $5 per person per night. Hikers making multiple trips into the canyon during a twelve month period may want to purchase a Frequent Hiker Membership for $25 in lieu of the $10 permit fee for each trip. Even with a backcountry permit, you will still need to pay the $25 entrance fee upon arriving at the National Park Entrance Station.

From left to right: Phantom Ranch Cantina, a cabin, and the dormitories.

For those of you interested in staying at Phantom Ranch: Built in 1922 Phantom Ranch is the only lodging facility below the rim and it can be difficult to obtain the required reservations, but this veritable oasis, located at the bottom of the Grand Canyon near the mouth of Bright Angel Canyon, is well worth the effort. A few of the rustic cabins not already reserved by mule trippers may be available for rent while the dormitories offer separate male and female accommodations. Meals must be booked at the same time as lodging, and reservations are accepted 13 months in advance. Making arrangements to stay at Phantom Ranch is the ideal choice for first-time canyon backpackers since you lighten your load considerably by not having to carry a tent, sleeping bag, and extra food (if you make meal reservations).

Phantom Ranch cabin prices are about $100, while the dorms are $27 per night. Meals are $15 for breakfast, $10 for box lunch, and for dinner, veggie or hiker stew is $18, while the steak dinner runs about $27.* You must check in at the Bright Angel Lodge Transportation Desk before setting off into the canyon, as they will provide the proper paperwork you will need when checking in at Phantom Ranch. The Cantina (or Canteen) is the check-in station at Phantom Ranch, as well as being the dining room, snack bar, and all around social gathering place for Phantom Ranch and Bright Angel campers. Those camping at Bright Angel Campground are welcome to reserve meals at Phantom Ranch to lighten their backpack load by at least a meal or two.

*All prices quoted in this book are approximate, do not include tax, and are subject to change.

Camping and Lodging

Camping within the National Park above the rim or along the Central Corridor trails is restricted to designated campgrounds with a limit of two nights at each campground, except from November 15th to February 28th, when there is a four-night limit. Also, more permits are available for small groups (maximum of 6 people) than for large ones (7 to 11 people) because there are few group sites. So remember when applying that limiting your group size greatly improves your chances for receiving a permit.

You have a lot of choices for camping and lodging before and after your trip below the rim. **On the South Rim** there are two National Park Service (NPS) campgrounds, Mather Campground is

Side Step: What Time Zone is the Grand Canyon?

The State of Arizona remains on Mountain Standard Time (MST) and does not change to Daylight Saving Time, except on the Navajo Reservation. Therefore, in the winter months, Arizona time is two hours earlier than Eastern Standard Time (EST), and in the summer, Arizona is three hours earlier than EST. California, (Pacific Standard Time) on the other hand, is one hour later than Arizona in winter and then shares the same time as Arizona in the summer.

Bright Angel Lodge.

located in Grand Canyon Village and is open year-round. It offers both tent and RV camping (with no hook-ups and a maximum 30-foot length). If traveling between April and November, you are advised to make reservations, which are accepted up to five months in advance. The Trailer Village adjacent to Mather Campground offers RV sites with hook-ups for about $25 per night and also has a dump station during summer months. At the east entrance into the park, Desert View Campground is open from mid-May until mid-October and operates on a first-come, first-served basis (no shower facilities and no hook-ups). The cost for either campground runs about $18 per night. Ten-X Campground is about two miles south of Tusayan, and sites run $10. Dispersed camping is allowed in some areas of the national forest along the North and South Rims, but restrictions apply. Contact the Kaibab National Forest for information.

Bright Angel Travel Desk.

South Rim lodging can be found inside the park at El Tovar ($135-$305), Bright Angel Lodge (standard lodge room, $55-$70); cabins, ($90-$145), Kachina Lodge or Thunderbird Lodge ($125-$135), Yavapai Lodge ($95-$115), or Maswik Lodge ($80-$125). There are several other commercial lodging options available in the town of Tusayan near the south entrance into the park.

Other South Rim services include various restaurants available at many of the lodges and outside the park in Tusayan (just outside the park's south entrance). Shower and laundry facilities are next to Mather Campground, while groceries and other supplies are sold in the General Store at Market Plaza, which also has camping equipment for sale or rent and limited gear repair services. There is a small general store at Desert View, and in Tusayan there is also a small grocery store.

Mather Campground entrance, South Rim.

The North Rim is essentially closed from mid-October through mid-May. This includes the North Rim Campground. Campsites (dump station, no hook-ups) run about $20. Reservations are required and can only be made a maximum of five months in advance, although you can check for last-minute cancellations if you're in a pinch.

Other seasonal camping located outside the park includes De Motte Campground ($12), Jacob Lake Campground ($12), and the Kaibab Camper Village (tent site, $12; site with hookups, $22; and rooms priced at about $65).

The only in-park lodging on the North Rim is at the Grand Canyon Lodge ($100-$130) and rooms are booked well in advance. The next closest lodging can be found 18 miles from the park entrance at Kaibab Lodge (rooms or cabins, $85-$125), or at the junction of Highway 89A and Route 67 at the Jacob Lake Inn ($90-$120).

Other services at the North Rim include dining at the Grand Canyon Lodge dining room, where making early reservations is highly advised, or at the snack bar. Both Kaibab Lodge and Jacob Lake Inn also have restaurants. Groceries and camping supplies can be purchased at the General Store next to the campground, while laundry and shower facilities are located in the same vicinity.

Remember that between mid-October and mid-May no gasoline, food, or lodging is available inside the park at the North Rim, and roads are not plowed.

When planning your transportation for a Rim-to-Rim backpacking trip you basically have two options. You can drop one vehicle off at the trailhead and then drive a second vehicle to the opposite Rim to start your hike or take the only shuttle available between each rim, the Trans-Canyon Shuttle ($65 per person, see page 85). The shuttle operates between mid-May and mid-November (one trip each way daily) and reservations are required. Of course you could just backpack from rim to rim, and then turn around and hike back to the rim where you parked. That would obviously make for a very long journey, but I have known some people who have done just that.

Please note that pets are not allowed into Grand Canyon below the rim. Above the rim they must be leashed at all times and cannot be left unattended, so please leave your pets at home or you'll have to make plans to board them at the kennel (see page 85) on the South Rim during your time hiking or backpacking.

The Park Service advises backpackers parking a vehicle on the South Rim to leave their secured vehicle at the Backcountry Information Center parking lot and take the shuttle to the trailhead. On the North Rim you can park at the North Kaibab Trailhead.

The North Rim Visitor Center is located next to Grand Canyon Lodge at the end of the North Entrance Road (Route 67).

Ten Essentials for all Hikes

☐ Water: I take a minimum of one quart for every hour of hiking, keeping a sport drink mixture with electrolytes in at least one bottle. You'll need more when going uphill—and even more in the summer.

☐ Food: I take mostly energy bars and salty trail mix for the trail and dehydrated meals for camp.

☐ First-Aid supplies: Be sure to include blister treatments and ibuprofen.

☐ Compass: Know the basics of how to use it.

☐ Topographic map of the area

☐ Detailed trail description

☐ Sunglasses, sunscreen, and a wide-brimmed hat (make sure to use them all!)

☐ Lightweight flashlight

☐ Loud plastic whistle

☐ Extra clothing

Detailed List for Backpackers

◉ Food and Water

☐ Water bottles: I take a 2-liter bottle and a 1-liter, wide-mouthed bottle filled for the trail, plus a collapsible bottle for camp.

☐ Water purification: For those times when the water pipes fail (which happens quite often).

☐ Food: About 2 pounds per day for each person.

☐ Backpack stove: Lightweight canister type.

☐ Cooking pot with cover: Titanium is light, but expensive.

☐ Fork and spoon: Plastic or titanium.

☐ Trash bag: A large sealable plastic bag will usually do.

☐ Drinking cup

◉ Shelter

☐ Tent: Lightweight—no more than eight pounds for a two-person tent.

☐ Sleeping bag: Temperature rated to match your hiking season.

☐ Sleeping pad: Therm-A-Rest, foam, or air mattress.

◉ Clothing

☐ Hiking boots: Lightweight, with good ankle protection, and well broken-in.

☐ Socks: I always wear a thin synthetic liner sock with a heavier wool or synthetic outer sock.

☐ Hat: Wide-brimmed for sun protection.

☐ Shirt and pants: Lightweight, comfortable layering, appropriate to the season (fleece in the cool season and cotton in the summer).

☐ Underwear: Comfortable, preferably synthetic or silk.

☐ Insulated jacket: Poly-filled or fleece.

☐ Camp shoes: Lightweight sandals or tennis shoes for off-trail comfort.

☐ Rain coat or poncho

☐ Gloves

◉ Hygiene

☐ Toilet paper: Provided at campgrounds, although they seem to run out regularly.

☐ Toothbrush & toothpaste

☐ Small lightweight towel

☐ Anti-bacterial hand sanitizer and/or biodegradable soap, anti-bacterial wipes.

☐ Lip balm

◉ Emergency

☐ First-Aid kit: A good comprehensive kit that includes a basic first-aid book. If you or anyone else in your group is allergic to insect bites, the kit should include an EpiPen, and everyone should know how to use it.

☐ Repair kit: Duct tape, plastic ties, light wire, nylon twine, nylon repair kit, sewing kit, and safety pins.

☐ Signal device: I carry a tin camping mirror.

☐ Waterproof matches and/or lighter

◉ Miscellaneous

☐ 10-20 feet of rope: To hang your packs.

☐ Bug repellent: Be sure to keep DEET off your skin and Gore-Tex type fabrics.

☐ Small pocket knife

☐ Watch or timepiece

☐ Extra batteries

☐ Pen or pencil

◉ Optional

☐ Hiking staffs: They give you stability and literally take tons of weight from your knees and ankles.

☐ Snake bite kit: Sawyer Extractor is recommended.

☐ Pillow

☐ Camera and film

☐ Rain pants and pack cover

☐ Other: _____

_____

_____

Note that this list may be reproduced by the reader as necessary.

Chapter Three

Rules and Tips

I must leave it as beautiful as I found it. Nothing must ever happen there that might detract in the slightest from what it now had. I would enjoy it and discover all that was to be found there and learn as time went on that here perhaps was all I ever hope to know.

Sigurd Olson

1. **Drink plenty of fluids.** Especially in the summer season you will need to drink at least a quart of water and/or sport drink for every hour of hiking. Soak your clothes, if possible, to keep cool, especially your hat, bandanna, and hair too.

2. **Rest often.** Break every hour for about ten minutes. Lie down and put your legs up if possible. Drink and eat snacks (especially salty snacks). Make sure to check that you have all your gear and trash before heading on.

3. **Take your time.** If you're unable to carry on a conversation and find yourself out of breath, slow down or you could suffer exhaustion and leg fatigue from the resulting lack of oxygen.

OK, let's get the Basic Rules out of the way...

Never go into the canyon unprepared. Make sure you are carrying enough water, food, sun protection, good hiking shoes, and adequate clothing layers. Ample water is a necessity. In summer months you must employ a sound strategy for limiting exposure to the midday heat. In winter months, the top 500 feet of the trail is usually icy, so make sure you have cleats or lightweight crampons to avoid a possible slip and fall. In summer, wear cotton clothing. In winter, wear fleece and synthetics that dry quickly. Always dress in layers.

Never attempt to go from the rim to the river and back in the same day. To hike round-trip from the canyon rim to the Colorado River in a day, especially in the heat of summer, is foolhardy and initiates many emergency rescues each year.

Redbud tree in bloom at Phantom Ranch.

Never hike alone. Although as an experienced backpacker I have hiked alone many a time in the canyon, it is especially advised for the first-time hiker not to hike alone. Statistics reveal that solo hikers make especially bad decisions when simple dehydration sets in. Also, be sure to tell someone else (who is not going on the hike) when to expect your return and what your itinerary is.

No swimming in the river. People have died trying to swim across the Colorado River. The current looks passive—until you are in the river and being swept downstream.

Never throw rocks. There is always the chance you might hit another hiker or camper, or even start a small rock slide.

Fed is dead. Feeding human food to wild animals can alter their digestive systems and ultimately kill them. It is also illegal to approach or feed any of the wildlife within the National Park, including deer or squirrels.

No fires are allowed in the backcountry.

The River Resthouse on Bright Angel Trail. Restroom facilities are scheduled to be installed at this resthouse and at Three-Mile Resthouse, at some future date.

Stay on the trails. Never shortcut switchbacks. It is illegal, very dangerous, and can easily cause rock slides. Plus, it causes erosion in a desert climate where plants have a difficult enough time getting established. Lack of vegetation, in turn, causes washouts on the trail during severe storms.

Also, keep your eyes on the trail. While you are hiking, your gaze should be glued to the trail just about three to six feet in front of you, with only quick glances further ahead to see what's coming up. You can take quick looks around, but keep your focus on the trail.

Pack it in, pack it out. Repackaging your food can help to minimize waste. Before you leave your campsite, or when you take a break on the trail, check and make sure you haven't left any food, litter, or hiking accessories. Before heading out after a trail break make sure your backpack or day pack is fully zipped and battened down. Once pack zippers start to open, they usually slide more, until they are wide open and you start dropping gear along the trail.

Pets are allowed only in developed areas above the rim, must be leashed at all times, and never left unattended.

Do not walk on cryptobiotic soils. These patches, which look like a fairly thick, black, hairy mold or lichen on the ground, help fix nitrogen in the soils for the establishment of plants. They are extremely fragile, and if you step on them it will take a long time to repair the damage. If you step off the trail for any reason, please make sure you don't step on these building blocks of the desert soil.

Bicycles are allowed only on maintained roads.

Graffiti is illegal. Respect other hikers' rights to a natural experience. Don't carve your name on anything, draw or doodle on the rocks, or build structures of any kind. And please suppress the need to write your latest snappy saying on the walls of the toilets. No one really cares to read your crass wit, and it simply adds to the backlog of maintenance chores for the park rangers.

Trail protocol. The uphill hiker has the right of way, but use common sense. Many times the uphill hiker welcomes a quick rest stop.

If a mule team approaches from either direction, step off to the inside of the trail, stand quietly, and wait until the last animal is at least 50 feet past before reentering the trail. Do not get yourself into the position where you are teetering on the outside edge of the trail waiting for a mule train to pass.

Food should be immediately placed in the storage container provided at each campsite. Otherwise, at the first chance they get, CRITTERS WILL CHEW INTO YOUR GEAR just to get to any accessible food scraps. Backpacks should be hung immediately on the posts provided, and all food items removed. If you leave any food inside, the birds will peck through your pack cloth to get to the food. The Grand Canyon is one of the worst backcountry areas for mice, deer, ringtails, raccoons, and various birds seeking food. If you leave any food unattended for even a couple of minutes, expect to have it eaten.

Respect other hikers trying to enjoy the natural environment. Avoid yelling or making loud noises on the trail or at your campsite.

Keep your permit on your person and easily accessible while hiking (usually secured to the outside of the group leader's backpack). When making camp, ensure that the permit is in plain view, as park rangers will come by at least once during your stay to check for proper permits.

 ## Side Step: Feeding the Deer

OK, this is still my first time in the canyon. (I learned quite a few lessons the first time in-canyon.) I'm with six people who have never been in the canyon, ranging in age from about 55 to 14 years old. After we wake from napping, exhausted after our hike to Bright Angel Campground from the South Rim, we sit and gobble dried fruit. Soon one person in the group notices a small herd of mule deer behind our camp, and a couple of people decide to feed the deer some dried fruit (something that is illegal to do). And it's kinda cute, taking pictures with the deer eating out of their hands. One of the young kids has a bag of dried fruit. He is talking and taking his time before handing out more food. One of the deer, adorable as it had appeared, decides the kid is taking too long and suddenly rears up and kung-fu kicks him right in the hip, just a few inches shy of the groin. It was a beautiful move, better than I'd ever seen Bruce Lee do, and it knocks the kid on his butt. Well, the rest of the group quickly decided the deer were probably satiated with dried fruit and they would stop feeding them. During the rest of the trip, he never would show us the black-and-blue bruise he got when, as we teased him, "Bambi kicked his ass."

Remember: The cliché "Fed is dead" means that feeding wild animals habituates them to interact with humans, which usually ends up harming the animal. It can cause injury to those feeding the animals, and hurt the animals themselves from being fed a diet of our processed foods. Keep a clean camp too! Even plastic bags with a slight scent of food will be eaten by the deer, and it really messes up their digestion.

Red rock formation past the Tip-Off along South Kaibab Trail.

Hiking and Backpacking Tips

Planning your hike: Two Central Corridor trails lead from the South Rim to Bright Angel Campground and Phantom Ranch, and one of the first questions I've heard people ask is, "Which trail should I take, Bright Angel or South Kaibab?"

Hmm, not an easy decision, but my personal preference is to go down the South Kaibab Trail, stay a couple nights at Bright Angel Campground, then up Bright Angel Trail to Indian Garden Campground (making sure to get out to Plateau Point for sunset), and finally up the remainder of Bright Angel Trail to the South Rim, for a total of four days (three nights). In planning your trip remember that the South Kaibab Trail, although three miles shorter than Bright Angel Trail, has no water and is very open and exposed to the sun. If you must plan your trip to hike out from the bottom of the canyon in one day, especially during the summer, you are best advised to hike up to Indian Garden in the early morning, rest under the tall cottonwood trees until later in the afternoon, then hike out as the trail gets more shade and temperatures begin to cool.

My favorite backpack trip through the Central Corridor of Grand Canyon is the classic rim-to-rim hike. You start from the North Rim, camp at Cottonwood Campground, then hike down along Bright Angel Creek past Phantom Ranch to camp the second night at Bright Angel Campground, then up to Indian Garden Campground for the final night, and out the next day. Of course, you could also travel in the opposite direction, taking the shuttle from the North to South Rim. The logistics may seem a little tougher when planning rim-to-rim trips, but this route is the quintessential canyon journey. Several other itineraries for Central Corridor backpacking trips are possible by scheduling more than one night at any given campground.

The National Park Service provides a free informational DVD for first-timers once your permit has been processed. Make sure you review the video and discuss the proposed route with all the hikers in your group. Plan together for the trip, and you can lighten the loads you carry: if one person wants to take the water filter, another can take the repair kit, etcetera. You will also want to verify the sunrise and sunset times (see page 36) to help you avoid hiking in the middle of a summer day.

Physically preparing for your hike: The average time from the South Rim to the Colorado River is about four to five hours down and nearly double that coming out. This makes for a long day, and you must ensure that you are physically ready to endure this activity with proper preparatory exercise.

Begin your conditioning several months in advance by doing step aerobics or hiking that involves enough elevation gain to steadily increase your heart rate, lung capacity, and muscle endurance. Start with short distances and increase the length of time

Bright Angel Point, North Rim.

Morning sun hits the canyon floor with Bright Angel Bridge in the foreground.

for these aerobic activities while simultaneously starting light and steadily increasing the amount of weight you take on, working up to a minimum of half the weight you intend to carry (I use a day pack and add weight by way of bricks.) Of course, be sure to check with your doctor for advice before beginning a new exercise regimen.

Shoes and foot protection: Your shoes should be constructed of lightweight, flexible materials, and must be thoroughly broken-in before venturing into the canyon. For desert hiking, there is no need for full-leather, stiff shank boots. I've also read that every extra pound of weight on your feet equals almost five pounds on your back, so it pays to be weight conscious about your feet.

One pair of mid- or heavy-weight socks should be worn. Some folks, like me, still use a lightweight inner sock for added cushioning. Socks should be made of wool or synthetic fabric, since cotton keeps feet wet and encourages blistering. I also use blister-blocking adhesive bandages for protection; my system is to apply one pair on the balls of my feet for going down the trail and another pair on my heels going up. I also brush some Liquid Skin on the area before I apply the bandages; it helps them stick and provides an extra layer of protection. Trim your toenails a few days before your trip to prevent long nails from cutting into adjacent toes and to give them time to heal in case you've trimmed them a little too close. I also wear short ankle gaiters to keep sand and rocks from getting into my shoes.

Classic Grand Canyon views can be found along the Tonto Plateau.

In addition, make sure you have plenty of room in your shoes for your toes; otherwise you can suffer from the common canyon malady, black-toe. This is a very painful condition caused when your toes constantly bang against the toe-box of your shoes, causing blisters and black-and-blue tootsies. It also helps to seat your heel well into the back of your shoes and tighten your laces a bit more (not too tight or you can cause circulation problems) before heading down into the canyon.

Water purification: Many people see clear water in a wilderness area and, believing it is safe, drink water freely from the creeks and rivers. What you can't see are things like giardia and cryptosporidium that can and will make you very sick! Although drinking water is provided at the campgrounds and most rest houses, due to pipeline breakage (which happens many times each year), and the fact that many water sources are turned off between October and April, you should carry an alternate way of purifying your water.

The most readily available method of purifying water for drinking and cooking is by boiling. This can be very time (and fuel) consuming, but heating water until it boils will kill anything harmful. Another choice is to use chemical treatments like Micropur or Potable Aqua systems. These are small and easy-to-carry chemical tablets that, when mixed into the water and allowed their allotted time, kill most contaminates. I still use a water filter. MSR, PUR, Katadyn, and Sweetwater all make excellent filters. Go for a lightweight system and ask your outdoor retailer for advice on which will work best for you. The newest forms of water treatment units are battery operated. One uses salt and electricity, and another works by using ultraviolet light. Both meet EPA guidelines.

Food basics: I readily admit that I am no gourmet, but unless you really need to cook extravagant meals, stick to the basics. Dehydrated meals made especially for backpacking and good old ramen-type noodles should suffice for most meals. For breakfast, I take instant oatmeal or similar dehydrated mixes that require just a little hot water to prepare. If you back that up with your choice of energy and nutritional bars, trail mixes, crackers, cheese, peanut butter, dried fruit, pretzels, or other salty snacks, then you should survive. Remember, the average hiker should consume about two pounds of food per day. If you eat meat, try sticking to chicken or turkey since beef and pork products can be harder to digest, feeling like a rock in the middle of your gut when hiking the next day and probably making you a little sluggish. Keep your food limited to one larger food bag and a small sealable plastic bag that can be readily accessed for snacking on the trail. As soon as you make camp, take both food bags and immediately store them in the food storage (ammo can) containers provided at each campsite.

While at the bottom of the canyon, you can save some backpack weight by scheduling meals at Phantom Ranch. It can be tricky to reserve a spot (breakfast, sack lunches, or dinner), but it is worth its weight in gold to eat a "home-cooked" meal, especially dinner, in the middle of your trip.

Backpacks: Internal frame packs are what most people use these days. They hug your back and have less side-to-side sway than external packs, giving you more stability. External frames keep the load off your back and provide some air flow between your back and the pack itself, making them a little cooler but slightly less stable from shifting loads. Externals allow you to walk more upright and are usually less expensive than internals but can be bulkier.

When backpacking, first of all, travel light. Food and water should be your two heaviest items, and you should only carry about one-third your total body weight when your backpack is fully loaded. When loading your backpack, make sure you pack most of the weight in the center of your back. This means that your heaviest item (usually the food bag), will be in the lower depths of your pack, so be sure to keep some nibble foods in a small bag readily accessible for snacking on the trail.

The usual order I use in packing, from bottom to top: sleeping bag, tent, food, miscellaneous, and clothing. Water bottles should be readily accessible while hiking, and I always keep rain gear or extra clothing layers at the top of the pack for quick access. You can adjust your pack to your liking, but make sure it is balanced from side to side. Try not to have loose straps that can get snagged along the trail, and don't stack your pack too high or you could find yourself bouncing dangerously off of tree branches, rock overhangs, and the like.

View from Bright Angel Bridge looking west.

With an internal frame pack, be very careful not to pack anything hard sticking into your back or stuff the pack to the point where the natural contoured shape of the pack is pushed out of kilter. The weight of your pack should ride on your hips. If the pack straps are cutting into your shoulders, tighten the hip belt around your waist or reach up to the straps near your ears and tighten the load lifters. When lifting your pack, use the haul strap located between the shoulder straps. Once when I was in Alaska, a guy transferring my gear onto a float plane carried my pack by using one shoulder strap. I subsequently spent the first night in the wilderness sewing the shoulder strap back on where the stitching had ripped from the stress. Finally, avoid additional stress on the pack by only tightening the straps until they are taut. Excessive tightening will cause seams to pop open eventually.

Sleeping bags: Down-filled bags are light and warm but can be expensive—and if they get wet, they lose their loft and are nearly useless. Synthetic bags will maintain some warmth when wet and are less expensive than down but will weigh a little more. Remember to match the bag's warmth rating with the season. Temperatures at night inside the canyon during the summer are around 80 degrees, so you won't need much. (I've used just a "cocoon" bag liner made of cotton, flannel, or fleece for summers in the Southwest.)

Hiking staffs (trekking poles): You'll hear some people call them ski poles and make dumb comments, but they literally take tons of weight off your knees for each mile you hike. For the unparalleled stability they provide, most backpackers are much better off using them. Ask your outdoor retailer which style suits you best and get used to them while preparing for your hike. If you choose not to acclimate yourself to using your trekking poles before your hike, you run a greater risk of tripping over them during your hike. Believe me, this is not the thing to do when hiking the canyon. If you do fall while hiking the canyon, always fall uphill, and try to keep your balance to ensure that you do not fall forward—your butt bounces much better than your head does!

Pace yourself and take breaks: The National Park Service recommends that your uphill pace should allow you to walk and talk without huffing and puffing. That could mean a very slow hike out, but remember that gasping for air equals inefficient use of energy reserves that in turn builds up the waste products that can make you feel sick. Go your own pace, but don't exceed your limits of exertion. Every hour you should take a break for five to ten minutes, take the pack off, and even put your feet up if you can. Take an extra drink, nibble some food, relax, and enjoy the views. Your body will thank you.

Know what temperatures to expect: Remember that even when temperatures are cool on the rims, Inner Canyon temps are going to be much warmer. Know the weather forecast, make sure you pack for the minimum and maximum temperatures you are likely to experience, and expect the worst-case scenario.

Average Temperatures for the Inner Canyon
(Subtract about 20 degrees to estimate temps on the Rim.)

	Jan	Feb	Mar	Apr	May	Jun	Jul	Aug	Sep	Oct	Nov	Dec
Highs (F)	55°	60°	70°	80°	90°	100°	105°	105°	100°	85°	70°	60°
Lows (F)	35°	40°	50°	55°	60°	70°	80°	75°	70°	60°	45°	35°

Average Precipitation for the Inner Canyon*

	Jan	Feb	Mar	Apr	May	Jun	Jul	Aug	Sep	Oct	Nov	Dec
In Inches	0.70	0.75	0.8	0.5	0.35	0.3	0.85	1.5	1.0	0.65	0.45	0.9

* Please note that some of the highest rainfall averages are in July, August, and September.

Storms in these months are more likely to bring flash floods.
Make sure you stay out of canyon washes during storms!

Sunrise Times

January 1st	7:35 a.m.
January 15th	7:30 a.m.
February 1st	7:25 a.m.
February 15th	7:10 a.m.
March 1st	6:55 a.m.
March 15th	6:35 a.m.
April 1st	6:10 a.m.
April 15th	5:55 a.m.
May 1st	5:35 a.m.
May 15th	5:20 a.m.
June 1st	5:10 a.m.
June 15th	5:20 a.m.
July 1st	5:15 a.m.
July 15th	5:20 a.m.
August 1st	5:35 a.m.
August 15th	5:45 a.m.
September 1st	5:55 a.m.
September 15th	6:05 a.m.
October 1st	6:20 a.m.
October 15th	6:30 a.m.
November 1st	6:45 a.m.
November 15th	7:00 a.m.
December 1st	7:15 a.m.
December 15th	7:25 a.m.

Sunset Times

January 1st	5:25 p.m.
January 15th	5:35 p.m.
February 1st	5:55 p.m.
February 15th	6:05 p.m.
March 1st	6:20 p.m.
March 15th	6:30 p.m.
April 1st	6:45 p.m.
April 15th	6:55 p.m.
May 1st	7:10 p.m.
May 15th	7:20 p.m.
June 1st	7:35 p.m.
June 15th	7:40 p.m.
July 1st	7:45 p.m.
July 15th	7:40 p.m.
August 1st	7:30 p.m.
August 15th	7:15 p.m.
September 1st	6:50 p.m.
September 15th	6:30 p.m.
October 1st	6:10 p.m.
October 15th	5:50 p.m.
November 1st	5:30 p.m.
November 15th	5:20 p.m.
December 1st	5:15 p.m.
December 15th	5:20 p.m.

All times are approximate and have been rounded off. If you are planning to watch a sunrise or sunset be sure to arrive at your viewing point at least fifteen minutes before these times.

(Remember too that Arizona remains on Mountain Standard Time.)

Chapter Four

Trails and Maps

Until one is committed there is hesitancy, the chance to draw back, always ineffectiveness. Concerning all acts of initiative (and creation), there is one elementary truth, the ignorance of which kills countless ideas and splendid plans: that the moment one definitely commits oneself, then Providence moves too.

William H. Murray

37

Bright Angel Trail

Trail Overview

Length: One-way mileage is 9.3 miles from the trailhead to Bright Angel Campground.

Elevations: 6,850 feet (trailhead) to 2,450 feet (Colorado River). Total elevation net loss/gain is 4,450 feet.

Bright Angel Trailhead is located behind the West Rim/Hermits Rest bus stop.

Hiking Time: Usually four to six hours going down and double that time to come up.

Difficulty: Strenuous, some shade areas, limited water along the trail.

Views: Superb views although more restricted than the South Kaibab Trail. Plateau Point, a spur trail from Indian Garden, provides one of the most beautiful views of the Colorado River you will ever see—from a 1,200 foot vantage point.

Bright Angel Day Hikes:

Mile-and-a-Half Resthouse:
3 miles round trip - 2 to 4 hours

Three-Mile Resthouse:
6 miles round trip - 4 to 6 hours

Indian Garden:
9.2 miles round trip - 6 to 9 hours

Plateau Point:
12.5 miles round trip - 9 to 12 hours

See the Mileage and Elevation Chart on page 60 for distances of individual segments of the trail. (Refer to map on page 43.)

Bright Angel Trail is the most popular trail into the canyon. It was one of the original trails used by the Havasupai Indians to access the Indian Garden area where they were still farming when the national park was established in 1919. Nowadays hikers can pack the trail, ideally staying ahead of the mule trains going to, and coming from, the canyon bottom. Due to trail use by these mule trains, it can be dusty and quite smelly in certain areas. The biggest advantage for choosing this trail is the availability of water (spring through fall), some shade, and excellent views of the canyon.

Trail Description

The trailhead begins on the west side of Bright Angel Lodge, past Kolb Studio, near the Hermits Rest gate and bus stop, next to the stone corral used by the mules. There is limited parking near the lodge. The Park Service recommends parking in the lot adjacent to the Backcountry Information Office and taking the shuttle over to the trail's start, or you can simply walk the half-mile to the trailhead.

If walking to the Bright Angel Trailhead from the Backcountry Office parking lot, you'll want to follow the sidewalk along the railroad tracks to the north, turn left crossing the tracks, and head toward Maswik Lodge. Approaching the Lodge, the road and sidewalk curves right. Stay on the sidewalk, heading north toward the canyon rim. You will cross the railroad tracks a couple times and will arrive at the Hermits Rest gate and bus stop. The trailhead is behind the bus stop, next to the stone corral. It takes about ten minutes to walk from the Backcountry Office to Bright Angel Trailhead.

 Side Step: **What's In a Name?**

I've always found it interesting to find out how places received their accepted names, so I thought I'd include just a few of the names of places you will probably encounter during your Grand Canyon experience.

Bright Angel Trail was named after Bright Angel Creek, which extends from the Colorado River north along the North Kaibab Trail. It was the intrepid traveler John Wesley Powell who first named the creek from the lyric of a hymn he recalled after camping there during his 1869 expedition.

Both North and South Kaibab Trails are named after the Kaibab Plateau on the North Rim. This 9,000-foot plateau is the second-highest in the world. The origin of the word Kaibab comes from the Paiute Indians in reference to the canyon; it is aptly translated as "mountain lying down."

The mighty Colorado stretches from its headwaters in the mountains of Wyoming and Colorado. Its name is a Spanish term that roughly translates as "color red." Usually, the river runs a very pretty (albeit unnatural) bluish color most of the year because Glen Canyon Dam traps most of its sediments. After a good drenching rain, the river will return to its natural red-brown color, remaining that way for several days.

The trail descends immediately; be sure in winter months to bring ice cleats or light crampons for this upper section. Or you can purchase them at the Market Plaza General Store. Early in the descent, you will pass through the first of two tunnels and slowly, though always steeply, continue along until you reach the second tunnel a short time later. The trail begins its steeper and shorter series of switchbacks as you meander down toward the first rest stop, aptly named Mile-and-a-Half Resthouse. With toilets, water, and an emergency phone available, this is a good turn-around spot for those who only have about three hours to hike round trip.

After leaving Mile-and-a-Half Resthouse, continue your downward momentum for another 1.5 miles, passing the hairpin turn at two-mile corner. The trail becomes a bit more scenic as you reach the Three-Mile Resthouse. This is another turn around point for those having only enough time for about a five hour round-trip hike. Water is available in back of the structure. There are excellent views just beyond the resthouse, on the spur trail just past the water spigot.

The trail will become steeper once you pass the Three-Mile Resthouse, descending down an area of red rock switchbacks called Jacob's Ladder. Finally, once you're beyond those switchbacks, the trail will level out a bit during the last half-mile or so until you reach Indian Garden at 4.6 miles.

Indian Garden makes another good turn-around point for day hikers. There are several places to rest and have a picnic under the huge cottonwood trees before climbing back out of the canyon. Other amenities include drinking water, toilets, emergency phone, and a ranger station.

Three-Mile Resthouse.

For anyone wanting a very strenuous day hike that takes a full day and brings you to one of the most beautiful overlooks in the canyon, Plateau Point is a great destination. The point lies about 1.5 miles from Indian Garden. At nearly 12.5 miles round trip and over 3,000 feet of elevation change, this route as a day hike is only for those in excellent physical condition. The reward is a spectacular panorama of the Grand Canyon, including a view of the Colorado River moving some 1,200 feet below you. To find this spur trail, simply follow the signs from Indian Garden. The Plateau Point Trail forks to the left near the mule corral past the bathrooms. The trail basically follows the Tonto Trail. Where the Tonto veers off to the left (west), continue straight (north) on the trail toward Plateau Point. The trail ends at the vista. Water is usually available here. If spending the night at Indian Garden Campground, this is a "must do" trail for late afternoons. Make sure to be off the trail during the hottest time of the day, from 10 a.m. to 4 p.m., when day hiking to Plateau Point in the summer. Relaxing at Indian Garden is your best choice while waiting for the midday heat to subside.

Leaving Indian Garden, Bright Angel Trail heads to the right just past the information kiosk and rest benches. Keep Garden Creek on your left (west) as you move into a wonderful little canyon called the Tapeats Narrows. The trail follows the creek until it turns into a small waterfall that drops off to the side of the trail as the creek disappears for a while. Soon you'll be looking into the Devil's Corkscrew. This is an open, steeply descending series of switchbacks that eventually takes you down to the creek bed. Once through the Corkscrew, the trail follows along the Pipe Creek drainage. You'll see an old mining tunnel on the left (west), and the trail mellows out to a more level pace as it merges with Garden Creek in an area called Columbine Spring. In less than a half-mile you will reach the River Resthouse next to the creek and adjacent to the Colorado River at 7.6 miles. (There are no facilities, but there is an emergency phone, and water can be filtered from the river.) Although still commonly known as Bright Angel Trail, the River Trail actually begins at this junction, just past the resthouse.

The trail then veers to the right (east) along the Colorado for another 1.5 miles or so, until you reach the river at the Bright Angel (Silver) Suspension Bridge, built in the late 1960s. The mules do not use the Silver Bridge. When crossing, stop in the middle of the bridge for a second to feel the bridge swing and sway. The Ranger Station, water, and toilets are just around the corner from the Park Service mule corral at 9.1 miles. To reach Bright Angel Campground, follow the signs for another one-third mile as the trail eventually crosses Bright Angel Creek on a small footbridge, bears to the left, and heads north into Bright Angel Canyon. Once in the canyon, you'll cross another small bridge on the left (west) to enter the campground. Continuing another half-mile up the trail will take you to Phantom Ranch.

Map Key

Road	Colorado River	Campground
Railroad	Creek	Water
Gate	Intermittent Stream	Restroom
Rim=Green Canyon=Brown	Bridge	Resthouse
Lower Elevations= Darker Brown	Main Trail	Phone
Highway	Side Trail	Ranger Station
Route	Side Trail Continues (not for the novice)	River/Creek Confluence

Map is not to scale

Phantom Ranch (9.8 miles)

Bright Angel Creek

Bright Angel Campground (9.3 miles)

Colorado River

River Resthouse (7.6 miles)

Bright Angel (River) Trail

Bright Angel (Silver) Bridge (8.9 miles)

Plateau Point (6.25 miles)

Columbine Spring

Bright Angel Trail

Devil's Corkscrew (6.2 miles)

Tonto Trail

Tapeats Narrows

Tonto Trail

Plateau Point (Tonto) Trail

INDICATES Seasonal Water

Indian Garden (4.6 miles)

Garden Creek

Jacob's Ladder

Yavapai Point

Three-Mile Resthouse (3 miles)

Mather Point

Mile-and-a-Half Resthouse (1.5 miles)

NORTH

Bright Angel Lodge

Bright Angel Trailhead

Market Plaza

INDICATES the Confluence of the Colorado River and Bright Angel Creek

Amenities include:

SOUTH RIM
Grand Canyon National Park

South Entrance Road

43

South Kaibab Trail

Trail Overview

Length: One-way mileage is 6.8 miles from the trailhead to Bright Angel Campground.

Elevation: 7,250 feet (trailhead) to 2,450 feet (Colorado River). Total elevation net loss/gain is 4,800 feet.

Hiking Time: Usually three to five hours going down and double that time to come up.

Difficulty: Very strenuous, no water, no shade. Trail is much steeper than Bright Angel Trail due to its shorter length.

Views: Spectacular views—most trails follow side canyon drainages while the South Kaibab follows open ridges, providing some of the prettiest panoramic views in the park.

South Kaibab Trailhead is located near Yaki Point.

South Kaibab Day Hikes:

Ooh Aah Point:
1.5 miles round trip - 1 to 2 hours

Cedar Ridge:
3 miles round trip - 2 to 4 hours

O'Neill Butte:
5 miles round trip - 4 to 5 hours

Skeleton Point:
6 miles round trip - 5 to 6 hours

See the Mileage and Elevation Chart on page 60 for distances of individual segments of the trail. (Refer to map on page 48.)

The South Kaibab Trail is the second most popular trail into the canyon. Because the Bright Angel Trail was originally constructed as a private venture, which included paying a toll for its use, the National Park Service built the South Kaibab early in the twentieth century as free access into the canyon. The advantages of hiking this trail are the shorter length (nearly two miles less than Bright Angel) and the drop-dead gorgeous views into the canyon. The disadvantages include no water, no shade, and—because of its shorter distance and greater elevation change—this route is quite a bit steeper.

Trail Description

This trailhead starts from a spur road near Yaki Point. If traveling along the Desert View Drive, take the road to Yaki Point and then your first paved road on the left. The road curves around until it opens into the parking lot and ends. The trailhead is clearly marked near the northeast corner of the lot. NOTE: The Park Service has closed the road to Yaki Point to all private vehicles, and now requires that most hikers use the free shuttle bus to access this trail. Recommended parking is available in the lot adjacent to the Backcountry Information Office, where you can take a shuttle over to the trailhead. Some people are now parking in a small lot about 1.3 miles past the turn onto the Desert View Drive, just past the turn-off to Yaki Point (although this is actually a picnic area and hikers are not encouraged to park here). From this small parking area, hike along the road for about 0.7 miles (about ten minutes) to access the trailhead. The other option for getting to the trailhead is taking the free Hiker Shuttle, which picks up at the bus stop to the east of Bright Angel Lodge and at the Backcountry Information Office. The times for the shuttle change every month, so check *The Guide*, the informational newspaper you receive at the park entrance, for the current Hiker Shuttle schedule. (For example, in summer months the "hiker express" shuttle starts running at 4 a.m. from the

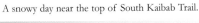
A snowy day near the top of South Kaibab Trail.

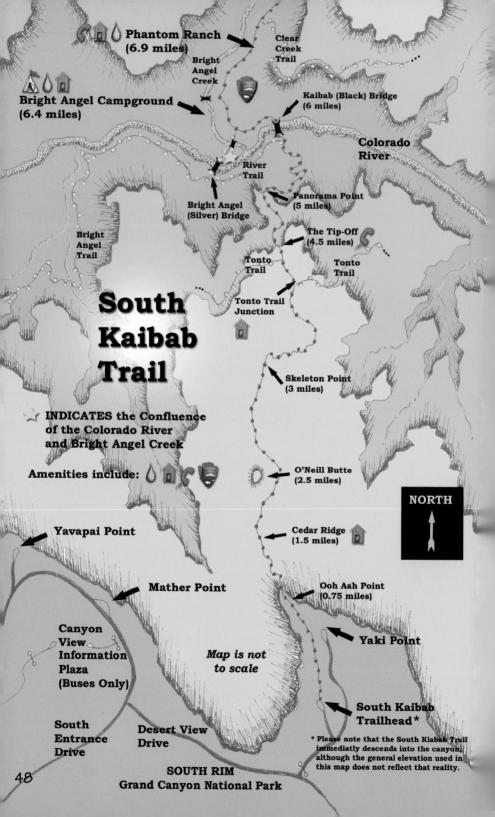

Phantom Ranch
(6.9 miles)

Clear
Creek
Trail

Bright
Angel
Creek

Bright Angel Campground
(6.4 miles)

Kaibab (Black) Bridge
(6 miles)

Colorado
River

River
Trail

Bright Angel
(Silver) Bridge

Panorama Point
(5 miles)

Bright
Angel
Trail

The Tip-Off
(4.5 miles)

Tonto
Trail

Tonto
Trail

South
Kaibab
Trail

Tonto Trail
Junction

Skeleton Point
(3 miles)

★ INDICATES the Confluence
of the Colorado River
and Bright Angel Creek

Amenities include:

O'Neill Butte
(2.5 miles)

NORTH

Yavapai Point

Cedar Ridge
(1.5 miles)

Mather Point

Ooh Aah Point
(0.75 miles)

Canyon
View
Information
Plaza
(Buses Only)

Yaki Point

*Map is not
to scale*

South
Entrance
Drive

Desert View
Drive

South Kaibab
Trailhead*

* Please note that the South Kiabab Trail
immediatly descends into the canyon,
although the general elevation used in
this map does not reflect that reality.

48

SOUTH RIM
Grand Canyon National Park

Backcountry Office and next to Bright Angel Lodge.)

As with any trail into the canyon, the South Kaibab Trail begins its descent immediately and follows a fault line along the west side of Yaki Point. In about 0.75 miles, the trail opens to the east at Ooh Aah Point, taking in breathtakingly expansive views. This is an excellent day hike that can be done in a couple of hours, although it is a small, unmarked area with no water. After a nearly 1,100-foot drop and about 1.5 miles of trail, you reach Cedar Ridge. This is the turn around point for a majority of day hikers, since it has a fairly level area with beautiful views and toilet facilities (no water). As a day hike, this three mile round trip jaunt can take three to four hours to complete.

Once past Cedar Ridge, the descent isn't quite as severe. The trail continues to the east side of the ridge toward the prominent rock feature O'Neill Butte at about 2.5 miles. The trail heads north and remains a bit less demanding until reaching Skeleton Point (you'll see a sign and a hitching post) at 3 miles. You'll drop down from Skeleton Point to a spot where a slice between two rock walls provides a glimpse to the west as the deep switchbacks begin and drop quickly (and steeply) down toward the Tonto Plateau. After about a dozen switchbacks, there is a small aluminum sign that marks 3.5 miles from the South Rim and 3.8 miles to Phantom Ranch. The switchbacks continue down and slowly shift toward the north. The trail again levels out a bit as the bathrooms come into view off in the distance announcing the junction of the Tonto Trail at about 4.3 miles. The building looks quite stark, as it sits on the plateau with no trees or shade anywhere around it. There are toilets and a hitching post but no water. An emergency phone is just ahead at The Tip-Off (4.5 miles). This is the jumping-off point for the last big descent to the Colorado River.

A moderately steep decline begins again shortly past the Tip-Off, and you'll catch your first glimpse of the Colorado River. Passing through an area of red rock formations, the trail descends steeply and presents a couple of promontories where you can look down to the river. At about 5 miles the most spectacular of these trail turnouts, named Panorama Point, provides a wonderful view of the

confluence of the Colorado River and Bright Angel Creek. The surrounding rocks then turn a dark gray until you reach the last steep drop down a series of tight switchbacks, passing the River Trail Junction sign and into a short tunnel at about 6 miles along the trail. The tunnel brings you onto the Kaibab (Black) Bridge and across the Colorado River. From the bridge, it is an easy walk the last mile as the trail moves west and then curves north into Bright Angel Canyon. You will pass a small bridge on the left (south) that heads toward a restroom and past that, the Bright Angel (Silver) Bridge. Once in the canyon, you'll cross a small silver-sided bridge on the left (west) to enter the campground (signed). Continuing less than a half-mile up the trail will take you to Phantom Ranch.

View of the river just past the Tip-Off.

North Kaibab Trail

Trail Overview

Length: One-way mileage is 6.9 miles from the trailhead to Cottonwood Campground, or 14.5 miles to Bright Angel Campground.

N. Kaibab Trailhead, located along Route 67.

Elevation: 8,250 feet (trailhead) to 2,450 feet (Colorado River). Total elevation net loss /gain is 5,800 feet.

Hiking Time: Usually four to six hours to Cottonwood Campground and double that time to come up. Add another three to five hours from Cottonwood Campground to Bright Angel Campground.

Difficulty: Very strenuous, some areas of shade, limited water along the trail.

Views: Excellent, although somewhat restricted due to being in a narrow canyon for the first few miles.

North Kaibab Day Hikes:

Coconino Point:
1.5 miles round trip - 1 to 2 hours

Supai Tunnel:
4 miles round trip - 2 to 3 hours

Redwall Bridge:
5.4 miles round trip - 4 to 6 hours

Roaring Springs:
10 miles round trip - 7 to 9 hours

See the Mileage and Elevation Chart on page 60 for distances of individual segments of the trail. (Refer to map on page 54.)

North Kaibab Trail is the only maintained trail into the Grand Canyon from the North Rim, but due to the more isolated location and winter closure of the North Rim, this trail receives much less travel in comparison to South Rim trails. Please be aware that the mule riders also use this trail in the open season. It is also important to remember that the North Rim and North Kaibab Trail are essentially closed from mid-October through mid-May due to snow. Water and toilets are only available along the trail from May through September.

Bruce Aiken was born in New York's Greenwich Village where he studied art until he visited the Grand Canyon when he was twenty years old and became captivated by the canyon light. From 1973 until 2005 he, his wife, and their children lived near Roaring Springs, deep in the canyon off the North Rim, painting and tending the water pump house. Picking up groceries for this family meant hiking up the North Kaibab trail nearly six miles, grabbing the grub and returning via the same route. Bruce's extraordinary paintings speak to the heart of the canyon in intimate and vivid detail, and he has been featured on television and in print on many occasions. I met him once and he was very amiable. He would often come out and say hi when hikers stopped near the residence. You can visit his website and check out his paintings at www.bruceaiken.com. Rumor has it his job was phased out when the pump house was retrofitted to run automatically. The Aikens family willingly retired and relocated after 30 years in the canyon.

Redwall Bridge is nearly three miles from the North Rim.

Trail Description

The trailhead is located in the cool forest of the North Kaibab Trail parking lot, along Route 67 (AKA the North Entrance Road), about two miles north of Grand Canyon Lodge, and a half-mile from the North Rim Campground. If you're traveling south from the park entrance station toward the Rim, the trailhead is about eleven miles. Just past the turnoff to Cape Royal and Point Imperial, you will see a sign for the Kaibab Trail, and the parking area will be on your left. The North Rim Backcountry Office is about three-quarters of a mile from the trailhead parking lot. Turn right at the signage for the office (currently a small trailer; a new office is scheduled to be built near the campground by 2008). A shuttle is provided from the Lodge to the trailhead for a fee, and reservations should be made when checking in.

Consistent with all inner canyon trails, the North Kaibab Trail begins its steep downgrade immediately. You will also notice that even on a cold morning, you will quickly be peeling off layers as you enter the canyon and encounter the heat from lower elevations rising up to the rim. Descending through a mixed forest of aspen, pine, and Gambel's oak, you will reach the Coconino Overlook in less than 1 mile. This point is relatively easy to reach, although it is still a strenuous day hike. It is a good turn-around point for those who only have about an hour and a half to hike but want to get just a little taste of what canyon hiking entails. Plus, the overlook rewards you with a beautiful view into Roaring Springs Canyon.

Continuing another 1.2 miles south-southeast, and after dropping about 1,400 feet in elevation, you reach the Supai Tunnel. This is a good place to take a break since both water and toilet facilities are seasonally available. This is also a good turn-around spot for day hikers who have only a few hours to hike.

Past the tunnel, you drop steeply into the redwall area also known as Hell's Kitchen, where it gets hotter as shade gets more sparse and trees give way to shrubs such as manzanita, cliffrose, and mountain mahogany. You will spot the Redwall Bridge from these upper reaches, and after a steep descent, you'll eventually cross the bridge at 2.7 miles. Past the bridge the trail climbs briefly then descends gradually, reaching a distinct natural rock feature called The Needle at

Roaring Springs Waterfall

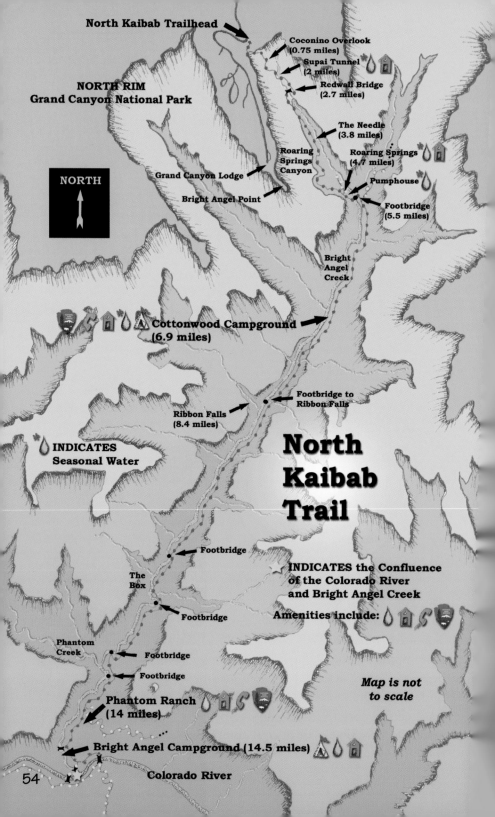

North Kaibab Trailhead

Coconino Overlook
(0.75 miles)

Supai Tunnel
(2 miles)

Redwall Bridge
(2.7 miles)

NORTH RIM
Grand Canyon National Park

The Needle
(3.8 miles)

Roaring
Springs
Canyon

Roaring Springs
(4.7 miles)

Pumphouse

Grand Canyon Lodge

Bright Angel Point

Footbridge
(5.5 miles)

NORTH

Bright
Angel
Creek

→ Cottonwood Campground
(6.9 miles)

Footbridge to
Ribbon Falls

Ribbon Falls
(8.4 miles)

⬤ **INDICATES**
Seasonal Water

North
Kaibab
Trail

Footbridge

The
Box

INDICATES the Confluence
of the Colorado River
and Bright Angel Creek

Footbridge

Amenities include:

Phantom
Creek

Footbridge

Footbridge

Map is not
to scale

Phantom Ranch
(14 miles)

Bright Angel Campground (14.5 miles)

Colorado River

54

about 3.8 miles. At this point you may begin to hear Roaring Springs. Continue on a generally southeastern course through Roaring Springs Canyon. At about 4.5 miles (and nearly 3,000 feet drop in elevation so far), Roaring Springs comes into view. A spur trail to the left at 4.7 miles takes you to a toilet, although drinking water will need to be filtered

The footbridge at Roaring Springs and Bright Angel Creek lies about 6 miles from the North Rim.

from the creek. Many people drop their backpacks at the junction to avoid humping them down and back from the facilities. There is also a day-use picnic area on the spur trail. This is the last turn-around for day-hikers since it is not recommended, or wise, to travel beyond the spring in a single day trip. It takes the average hiker seven hours or so to complete this 10-mile round-trip route.

From Roaring Springs, a relatively short hike leads you to the Pumphouse at 5.7 miles, where there is a picnic table and seasonal drinking water. The junction of Roaring Springs Creek and Bright Angel Creek is only a stone's throw from the Pumphouse. After crossing the creek on a small bridge, the trail mellows quite a bit and steadily moves south-southwest down Bright Angel Canyon, until you arrive at Cottonwood Campground at around the 7-mile mark. Water, toilets, and emergency phone are available on a seasonal basis (usually May through September). While most campsites provide little shade, there is an area next to the Ranger Station where you can relax and take refuge under the tall trees during the heat of midday.

Leaving Cottonwood Campground, the trail meanders in easy fashion south-southwest in a nearly straight line down Bright Angel Canyon. About 1.5 miles from Cottonwood Campground, there is a side trail off to the right (west) that crosses a small bridge to a beautiful little waterfall named Ribbon Falls. Everyone should make it a point to spend some time catching waterfall spray at this desert oasis, which is only about a half-mile from the trail.

Once back on Kaibab Trail, maintain your south-southwest direction for a few miles as the dark canyon walls start closing in on you and you enter an area known as The Box. Zigzagging through the canyon you'll cross a few bridges back and forth over the creek until you come to Phantom Creek, which flows in from the right (west). Looking up toward the south, you will also catch glimpses of Sumner Butte sticking up into the sky.

The final confirmation that you are near completion of this trail will be the sign at the junction of the North Kaibab and Clear Creek Trails. Keep going straight and finally, after over 14 miles and close to 6,000 feet altitude change since leaving the North Rim, you arrive at Phantom Ranch. Bright Angel Campground is a half-mile further. You'll cross a small bridge on the right (west) to enter the campground.

Agave plants bloom in bright yellow flower spikes along North Kaibab Trail.

Bright Angel / Phantom Ranch Day Hikes

Trail sign overlooking the Kaibab (Black) Bridge.

If you're going to be staying at Bright Angel Campground or Phantom Ranch for more than one night there are three good day hikes in the area: the River Trail, Clear Creek Trail, and the North Kaibab Trail to Ribbon Falls.

River Trail

This trail connects the South Kaibab Trail and Bright Angel Trail on the south side of the Colorado River. It's only about a mile or so in length, running between the Kaibab (Black) and Bright Angel (Silver) Bridges (although the River Trail technically runs the full length along the south side of the Colorado River until reaching the official Bright Angel Trail junction adjacent to the River Resthouse, nearly 1.5 miles west of the Silver Bridge).

Clear Creek Trail

This trail starts about a quarter-mile north of Phantom Ranch, where there is a sign marking its beginning. The trail heads right (east), and immediately starts to climb. There are a couple of overlooks down onto Phantom Ranch. A good day hike is to climb about 1,400 feet up to

View of the river from Clear Creek Trail looking east.

the Tonto Plateau (only a couple of miles) and explore the various vistas and rock formations, then return via the same route. It is not recommended to attempt hiking the full trail, which ends at Cheyava Falls (seasonal), in one day since it would mean a nearly 18-mile round-trip hike on a usually dry trail.

North Kaibab Trail to Ribbon Falls

This is a nearly twelve-mile round-trip day hike from Phantom Ranch to a beautiful waterfall nestled in the canyon walls. From Phantom Ranch, head north-northwest on North Kaibab Trail. Once you've passed Phantom Ranch coming in from the left (west), you will begin entering a narrow area of the canyon called The Box. After crossing a few bridges over the creek, the canyon will begin to open up. In about 5.6 miles, you'll see the waterfall off to the left (west) and an access trail that leads you into this wonderful alcove. Return via the same route.

Ribbon Falls is the epitome of the proverbial oasis in the desert.

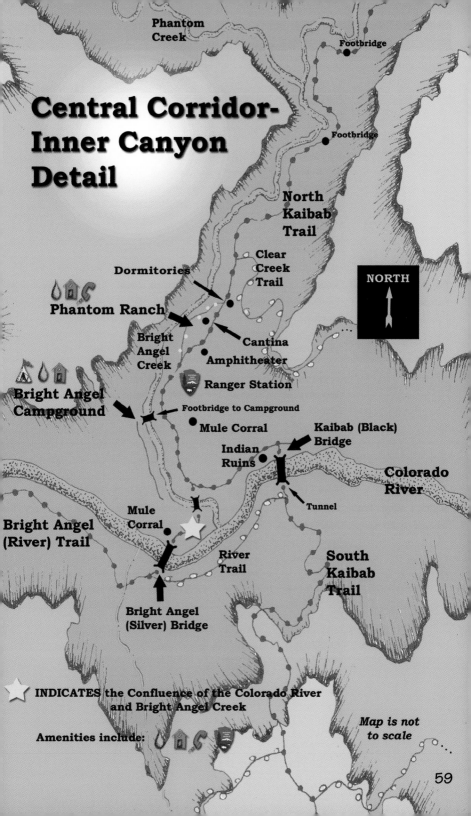

Central Corridor-
Inner Canyon
Detail

Phantom
Creek

Footbridge

Footbridge

North
Kaibab
Trail

Clear
Creek
Trail

Dormitories

NORTH

Phantom Ranch

Cantina

Bright
Angel
Creek

Amphitheater

Ranger Station

Bright Angel
Campground

Footbridge to Campground

Mule Corral

Kaibab (Black)
Bridge

Indian
Ruins

Colorado
River

Tunnel

Bright Angel
(River) Trail

Mule
Corral

River
Trail

South
Kaibab
Trail

Bright Angel
(Silver) Bridge

INDICATES the Confluence of the Colorado River
and Bright Angel Creek

Map is not
to scale

Amenities include:

59

Bright Angel Trail
Trailhead - 6,850 feet

Landmark	Miles from Rim	Elevation	Water	Toilets	Emergency Phone
1.5-Mile Resthouse	1.5 miles	5,700 feet	May-Sep	Yes	Yes
3-Mile Resthouse	3 miles	4,700 feet	May-Sep	No	Yes
Indian Garden	4.6 miles	3,800 feet	Yes	Yes	Yes
Plateau Point (Side Trail)	6.25 miles	3,800 feet	Usually	No	No
Devil's Corkscrew	6.2 miles	3,200 feet	No	No	No
River Resthouse	7.6 miles	2,500 feet	No	No	Yes
Bright Angel Bridge	8.9 miles	2,500 feet	No	No	No
Confluence of Colorado River & Bright Angel Creek	9.1 miles	2,450 feet	Yes	Yes	Yes
Bright Angel Campground	9.3 miles	2,450 feet	Yes	Yes	Yes
Phantom Ranch	9.8 miles	2,550 feet	Yes	Yes	Yes

South Kaibab Trail
Trailhead - 7,250 feet

Landmark	Miles from Rim	Elevation	Water	Toilets	Emergency Phone
Ooh Aah Point	0.75 miles	6,450 feet	No	No	No
Cedar Ridge	1.5 miles	6,300 feet	No	Yes	No
O'Neill Butte	2.5 miles	5,700 feet	No	No	No
Skeleton Point	3 miles	5,200 feet	No	No	No
Tonto Trail Junction	4.3 miles	4,000 feet	No	Yes	No
The Tip-Off	4.5 miles	3,850 feet	No	No	Yes
Panorama Point	5 miles	3,550 feet	No	No	No
Kaibab Bridge	6 miles	2,500 feet	No	No	No
Confluence of Colorado River & Bright Angel Creek	6.2 miles	2,450 feet	Yes	Yes	Yes
Bright Angel Campground	6.4 miles	2,450 feet	Yes	Yes	Yes
Phantom Ranch	6.9 miles	2,550 feet	Yes	Yes	Yes

North Kaibab Trail
Trailhead - 8,250 feet

Landmark	Miles from Rim	Elevation	Water	Toilets	Emergency Phone
Coconino Overlook	0.75 miles	7,600 feet	No	No	No
Supai Tunnel	2 miles	6,800 feet	May-Sep	Yes	No
Redwall Bridge	2.7 miles	6,250 feet	No	No	No
The Needle	3.8 miles	5,900 feet	No	No	No
Roaring Springs Junction	4.7 miles	5,200 feet	May-Sep	Yes	No
Pumphouse	5.7 miles	4,850 feet	May-Sep	No	No
Cottonwood Campground	6.9 miles	4,000 feet	May-Sep	Yes	Yes
Ribbon Falls	8.4 miles	3,750 feet	No	No	No
The Box	12 miles	2,950 feet	No	No	No
Phantom Ranch	14 miles	2,550 feet	Yes	Yes	Yes
Bright Angel Campground	14.5 miles	2,450 feet	Yes	Yes	Yes
Confluence of Colorado River & Bright Angel Creek	14.7 miles	2,450 feet	Yes	Yes	Yes

Chapter Five

Mishaps and Remedies

May your trails be
crooked, windy,
lonesome, dangerous,
leading to the most
amazing view.

Edward Abbey

I n any given year about a dozen people perish at the Grand Canyon. The most common medical problem you will possibly encounter in the canyon is blisters, followed by ankle injuries, knee complaints, and diarrhea, in that order. The list of all possible mishaps relevant to the hikers and backpackers goes something like this: cardiac arrest, getting lost, heatstroke, insect and snake bites, lethal falls, hypothermia, flash floods, drowning, rock slides, and lightning. Things happen, BUT, with proper preparation and a bit of common sense, you can lessen the chance of any of these things occurring.

In this chapter, I take the most common health and safety concerns that can occur in the canyon and provide a modicum of advice to help you avoid getting into troublesome situations and know what to do in case those things happen. This advice does not replace taking certified first-aid training. The National Outdoor Leadership School (NOLS) teaches wilderness first-aid courses throughout the country that provide excellent training (see Contact Information on page 85). I've taken the course and highly recommend it.

Storm clearing in March near Ooh Aah Point on the South Kaibab Trail.

Be sure you carry a suitable first-aid kit including ibuprofen, tweezers, and plenty of foot-care items. Any good outdoor first-aid kit, such as those offered by Adventure Medical Kits or Atwater Carey, will also include a first-aid booklet. You should take the time to read it thoroughly and practice before and during your trip.

IN ANY SITUATION...

Stay calm, take a deep breath, assess the situation, and take control. Do not rush in to help someone else before you make sure the scene is safe—adding

A moist grotto next to Ribbon Falls along the North Kaibab Trail.

another injured person does not help the situation. Do not move the victim unless he or she is in danger. Once everyone's safety is assured, then approach the victim and determine what has happened, or what is called the Mechanism of Injury (MOI). Talk to the victim to get a general impression of the situation, which could be anything from "I'll be all right," to "I think something's broken," to the victim's being totally unconscious. Try to write down your assessment and keep a record of the victim's condition. Again, review your first-aid book for details on this initial assessment and always have at least one person remain with the victim if additional help is required.

The National Park Service policy is to evacuate only under the most extreme circumstances, such as when the hiker's condition could turn critical if required to continue hiking in or out. A patient requiring rescue from the inner canyon puts many other people's lives at risk, so this should only be considered as a last resort. You should also be reminded that the hiker requiring emergency evacuation will be charged the cost of their rescue.

Check the patient's ABCs (use the first-aid book in your kit for complete details):

A. Airway—If the patient is conscious and choking, use the Heimlich maneuver to clear the obstruction. If unconscious and not breathing, check for obstructions in the mouth, and use the head-tilt, chin-lift method to open the airway. (If a spinal injury is suspected, use the jaw-thrust method).

B. Breathing—Once you have opened the airway, put your ear over the patient's mouth. Looking at the chest and abdomen for movement, listen for sounds of breathing, and feel for air against your ear. If the patient is not breathing on his or her own, you must initiate rescue breathing.

C. Circulation and bleeding—Listen for a heartbeat and check for a pulse. If none, you will have to initiate CPR. Next, while wearing protective gloves, check for bleeding. Visually inspect the patient and run your hand under bulky clothing, checking your hand for any sign of blood. To control bleeding, apply direct pressure with the palm of your hand and elevate the wound if possible.

D. Disability—If you suspect a lower limb fracture, a spinal injury (noticeable signs are immobility or tingling in hands or feet, for which you would cradle the patient's head and keep the neck from moving), or any other life threatening emergency, send someone for help as soon as possible while you stay with the victim. Make sure the messenger knows the exact location and the complete nature of the injury or situation.

E. Exposure—Keep the patient comfortable, sheltered from rain and cold, and treat for shock.

Blisters

Problem: Blisters are really burns caused by friction. Although they can be extremely painful, the main medical concern is infection. You can expect to get blisters hiking the canyon unless special precautions are taken to prevent them.

Prevention: Wear shoes that are broken in, use blister-blocking adhesives, treat hot spots immediately, and change into a pair of dry

socks during the hike. (See also Shoes and Foot Protection, page 29.)

Treatment: If you do get a blister, use a sterile pin or knife, open a small hole in the blister and massage out the fluid. Spenco 2nd Skin works best for covering blisters, and it aids in healing. (Just make sure you peel the plastic covering and apply the gel directly onto the blistered area.) Otherwise, cut a donut hole into moleskin and apply it so the blister is exposed through the hole. Put a small amount of triple antibiotic ointment (less is more) in the hole and cover with another bandage.

Cactus Spines

Problem: I have rested my pack against a small cactus or accidentally brushed against a prickly pear on numerous occasions. You'll normally find that the large spines are easily removed with a simple tug. It's those little spines, or glochids, that are the biggest nuisance. Barely perceptible, these little buggers are the ones that you can feel when you brush your hand against your skin but can't really see.

Prevention: Yes, good idea—avoid touching the cactus!

Treatment: The easiest way to remove glochids is with a pair of tweezers. With a dark background and the affected area in bright light, you can usually spot the difference between your own body hair and the straight, stiff, slightly thicker glochid. Once you spot it, just pluck it with your tweezers. If you can feel it but can't spot it, I recommend the shotgun approach. Narrow down the area and use the tweezers to repeatedly pick at the skin until you no longer feel

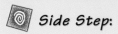
Major John Wesley Powell

If one were to choose the Grand Canyon's most iconic figure, it would have to be John Wesley Powell. Though by all accounts he was probably a jerk to work for, Powell was a veteran and hero of the Civil War who lost one arm during the battle of Shiloh. In 1869 he led the first expedition through the previously uncharted canyon with nine men in four wooden boats. Three members lost their lives when they decided to hike out, never to be seen again, and most of the expeditions gear was also lost as various rapids capsized the boats. They traveled through the canyon for nearly 100 days before emerging from its depths at the confluence of the Colorado and Virgin Rivers. A self-taught scientist and well-rounded individual, Powell would climb the canyon walls to help record the route, at one time getting caught hanging from a ledge. Another member of the party was required to remove his pants as a rescue rope to haul Powell up from what would have otherwise been certain death. Powell went on to form the U.S. Geological Survey and lobbied Congress on the dangers of developing extensive communities in the arid Southwest.

the spine. I've also heard that a piece of duct tape, applied to the affected skin and then pulled off, will remove these little spines.

Cardiac Arrest

Problem: The symptoms include chest pain; shortness of breath; nausea and vomiting; and pale, sweaty skin, among others.

Prevention: Most canyon hikers that have heart attacks on the trail have a previous condition that can be exacerbated by the strenuous activity. If you have a prior heart condition, be sure you have trained adequately for this arduous hike and get clearance from your doctor.

Treatment: General treatment includes keeping the airway open; keeping the patient still, calm, and comfortable; initiating CPR; and arranging rapid evacuation.

Dehydration/Muscle Cramps/Heat Stroke

Problem: After blisters, heat related ailments are the most common maladies in the canyon, bar none. Initial symptoms of dehydration include headache, pale and sweaty skin, muscle cramps, nausea and vomiting, and fatigue. If not treated heat stroke will set in, your skin will turn red and hot, and you will soon become disoriented, irritable, combative, and ultimately unconscious. A common nickname for cramping during the climb out of the canyon, is "Doing the Kaibab Shuffle." I have done the Kaibab Shuffle once, on a late September day hike from the North Rim to Roaring Springs and back. I wasn't fully prepared, I didn't take enough sport-drink mix, and it was 95 degrees by the time I got to the spring. It was a miserable feeling to have my legs seize up that way and be forced to take baby steps for the last mile.

The symptoms of dehydration and overheating get progressively worse as water loss increases. Remember that the human body is 60 percent water and a canyon hiker can lose 20 percent (or about 12 to 18 pounds) of that water in one day of hiking. The chronological order of heat-related injury for the average person goes something like this: After sweating about 2 percent of your body weight in water, your thirst mechanism is triggered. At 3 percent your performance is reduced by about 10 percent. Around 3 to 4 percent loss, heat exhaustion and muscle cramping set in. Then, at about 5 percent, your body begins losing a severe amount of muscle strength and endurance, and you begin to make really bad decisions. By the time your body has lost 6 to 9 percent of its water weight, incapacitation sets in, and you are unable to stand. Next comes the onset of total delirium and coma, and when you reach 20 percent, you are gone.

Prevention: Start drinking extra water a few days before your trip and use sport drinks with electrolytes a couple of hours before you begin your hike and while on the trail.

Bright Angel Creek from the campground bridge looking north.

Sport drinks containing electrolytes help keep your body chemistry balanced when sweating a lot. Especially in the summer season, you will need to drink nearly a quart of water and/or sport drink for every hour of hiking, and eat salty snacks. Drink enough fluids so that your urine runs clear and almost colorless, rest often while hiking, and rest during the heat of midday. Wear light-colored, lightweight, well-ventilated cotton clothing and wear a hat for shade and heat protection. Cotton, when soaked, stays wet for a long time. Therefore, in the summer you should wear a loose cotton shirt that will hold sweat and keep you cooler. Also, avoid alcohol and caffeine, and consult your physician if taking antihistamines, antidepressants, or other medications that may promote dehydration.

Treatment: Rest in a cool, shady spot. Slowly drink copious amounts of water and/or sport drinks. If symptoms progress, aggressive cooling is required. Spray the victim with cool water and fan him or her while massaging cramping as needed. Evacuate if incapacitated.

Drowning

Problem: Though the Colorado River appears to slowly meander through the canyon, a huge amount of water flows within the narrow constraints between its walls. Especially during the hotter seasons, some people think they'll just jump in and cool off for a minute and then are swept to their death downstream. Even if they survive long enough to climb out of the river, they are faced with the daunting chore of trying to find a way out of the canyon with no supplies, when trails are few and very far between.

Prevention: NEVER attempt to swim the Colorado River or go into the water much more than ankle deep. Do not overindulge in alcohol or other intoxicants while traveling the canyon. From what I've read, intoxication is one of the major circumstances for accidental river drownings.

Treatment: If the victim is unconscious, check for breathing and initiate rescue breathing if necessary. Check for a pulse and initiate CPR if necessary. Evacuate the victim as soon as possible.

You never know what you might run into - a bighorn sheep ambles up South Kaibab Trail.

Falls and Sprains

Problem: It will do you well to remember that in any direct fall of over twenty feet, you will break something, be it an arm or leg, or sustain a spinal or head injury. I once witnessed a father watch his two young boys climbing nearly forty feet up the rock walls, at dusk, in Bright Angel Campground. I knew if either boy were to fall he would have suffered injury and could probably not be evacuated until the next morning. Luckily, it didn't happen, but I still think about how irresponsible it was for the parent to allow it in the first place. It is impossible to review fully, in this short tome, the myriad traumatic injuries that can occur from a fall.

Prevention: Do not climb canyon walls unless you are highly trained. Even then, while in a remote wilderness setting, I would not put myself in a situation where these types of injuries could occur. When hiking, keep your eyes and concentration on the trail or you could easily trip and go tumbling butt over teakettle into the canyon.

Treatment: For simple sprains, RICE it. The acronym stands for Rest, Ice, Compression, and Elevation. So rest the injured area, apply ice or cold to decrease the swelling, wrap it, and elevate it. As already stated, the list of possible sprains, fractures, and other blunt-force trauma that can happen from a fall in the canyon is too

Looking up at the rim from under the Kaibab Bridge.

lengthy to be covered here. Please refer to your first-aid book for specific treatment, initiate the ABCs, and evacuate as needed.

Flash Floods

Problem: Flash floods kill more people in the United States each year than any other natural disaster. Just a few years ago a fellow photographer and highly experienced canyon backpacker from Flagstaff died in a canyon flood along with his hiking companion. Due to the steep, rocky terrain, any rainstorm is capable of producing flash floods at any time of year. In the Southwest during the summer monsoon season from late June to mid-September, afternoon thunderstorms are common. Be aware that these are the storms most likely to produce flash floods.

Prevention: Be cautious and stay away from creek beds, dry washes, and narrow canyons, especially in afternoons during monsoon season and during any rainstorms. If you hear or see a flood coming, immediately climb to higher ground. Never try to outrun it!

Treatment: Drowning and general trauma are the usual injuries resulting from a flash flood; treat the victim accordingly, initiate ABCs, and evacuate as needed.

Getting Lost

Problem: On the well-maintained trails described in this guide it is nearly impossible to get lost unless you really stop paying attention. All the same, I have seen people leave the trail and attempt climbing a wash, where they missed the upper trail completely. I have also seen people so engrossed in their conversation that they started descending a loose rock wash instead of the trail. These situations can cause an injurious fall or set in motion a serious rock slide that careens down the canyon causing injury to other hikers.

Prevention: As a general rule, if you are going down into the canyon, and you have a choice in direction where there is a fork in the trail, the main trail will nearly always descend, and vice-versa if traveling up out of the canyon. Always stay on the trail and never shortcut switchbacks. If the trail peters out, stop immediately, turn around, and retrace your steps back to the main trail. If you see a spur trail where you must step over broken branches or rocks to gain access, more than likely you will have just stepped off the main trail.

Treatment: Prepare by studying maps and trail descriptions before and during your hike. Learn basic compass and navigational skills prior to the trip. If you are totally and hopelessly lost in the canyon, stay calm and stay right where you are, using your whistle or signal device to let rescuers and others know your location.

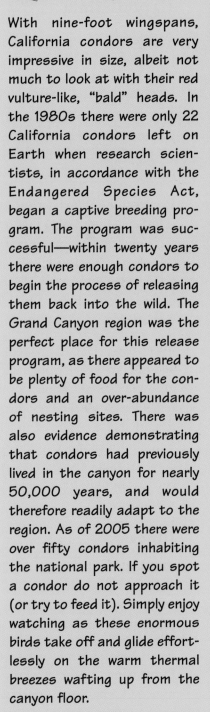

Side Step: Condors

With nine-foot wingspans, California condors are very impressive in size, albeit not much to look at with their red vulture-like, "bald" heads. In the 1980s there were only 22 California condors left on Earth when research scientists, in accordance with the Endangered Species Act, began a captive breeding program. The program was successful—within twenty years there were enough condors to begin the process of releasing them back into the wild. The Grand Canyon region was the perfect place for this release program, as there appeared to be plenty of food for the condors and an over-abundance of nesting sites. There was also evidence demonstrating that condors had previously lived in the canyon for nearly 50,000 years, and would therefore readily adapt to the region. As of 2005 there were over fifty condors inhabiting the national park. If you spot a condor do not approach it (or try to feed it). Simply enjoy watching as these enormous birds take off and glide effortlessly on the warm thermal breezes wafting up from the canyon floor.

Hypothermia

Problem: It is reported that hypothermia could be related to more backcountry injuries and deaths than any other cause. Basically, if your body loses heat faster than it can be produced, your body's core temperature will begin to plummet, and you'll begin to lose your head. Symptoms usually start with a loss of fine motor skills and total lack of judgment, followed by uncontrolled shivering and cold, pale skin. As this condition progresses, the victim stops shivering and ultimately loses consciousness.

Prevention: When temps are cool or cold, wear clothing layers (synthetics and fleece) that retain heat when wet. Be aware that cotton holds no heat when wet and stays wet for a long time, thus the cliché, "cotton kills." Use rain gear during inclement weather and change into warm, dry clothes as soon as you arrive in camp, before getting chilled. Drink lots of water, eat plenty of carbs, and rest often.

Treatment: Get the patient warm, dry, and sheltered from wind and rain. Make sure the head and neck are covered to prevent heat loss, and have the patient drink a warm (not hot) beverage. The old remedy is to use direct body contact to warm the victim, but this has recently been dismissed in lab tests. Instead, use heat packs or hot water bottles applied to the patient's palms and soles (but not directly on the skin), and get him or her wrapped into a sleeping bag, insulated from the ground, adding layers for extra warmth. Evacuate if necessary.

Illness

Problem: In this broad category, I'll quickly cover common illnesses such as headache, diarrhea, muscle aches, and sunburn. These are some of the typical maladies that can happen while hiking. I have experienced many of these problems myself, including a 24-hour stomach virus the night before hiking out.

Prevention: In the wilderness, diarrhea is usually caused by poor hygiene, so be sure to wash your hands after going to the toilet and before eating. Keeping a small bottle (0.5 ounce), of hand-sanitizing gel in my pocket seems to work well for me. Some problems can be difficult to avoid, but things like overexertion, a pack that's too heavy, and overexposure to the sun can all contribute to headaches and other body pains. Make sure you cover any exposed skin with either clothing or sunscreen and wear a wide-brimmed hat when out in the sun. (Anytime I hike the canyon I wear a "foreign legion" style cap with a large bill and a cape to cover my neck.)

Treatment: For headache and muscle aches, rest, drink water or sport beverages, use massage, and take a pain-killer such as ibuprofen. When sunburned, limit any added exposure, cool the skin, apply aloe or a skin moisturizer, and take a pain-killer such as ibuprofen. If subject to a bout of diarrhea, it is especially important to stay hydrated, so drink water and electrolyte-type sport drinks, and take an over-the-counter medication if necessary. There are also oral rehydration salt solutions that can be found in packet form at most outdoor retailers. These are best used for fighting the worst cases of diarrhea, and although their taste is not very appealing, be sure to include them in your first-aid kit.

During my bout of stomach virus, I had diarrhea, vomiting, and a mild fever all night. I kept myself hydrated using water with a little oral rehydration salt mixed in, and I took an anti-diarrhea medication. Since I hadn't slept, I crashed out in camp during the day, ate some oatmeal, drank until I could drink no more, took some aspirin, and headed up the trail that late afternoon. It wasn't the most fun I've had climbing out of the canyon but ya do whacha ya gotta do.

Bright Angel Trail near the Devil's Corkscrew.

View near the top of Bright Angel Trail.

Lightning

Problem: Second only to flash floods, lightning kills more people each year in the United States than any other weather-related incident. A single bolt can carry as much as 200 million volts and can strike a person up to ten miles away from the storm front.

Prevention: Familiarize yourself with the local weather patterns, such as the Southwestern summer monsoon season, which brings afternoon thunderstorms. Avoid hiking in exposed locations like cliff edges or being near isolated tall objects like trees and metal poles during these and other stormy times. In order to monitor a storm front, remember that sound carries at one mile per five seconds, so if you count the number of seconds after you see a flash of lightning and divide it by five, you'll know about how far away the storm is. If caught in a lightning storm, get to a low area that does not collect water, take off your pack, and squat low on your sleeping pad (for insulation), if possible. In your tent, stay on your sleeping pad and do not touch the tent walls. If at any time you feel the hair rise on the back of your neck, get down quick!

Treatment: A lightning strike can accost hikers in many ways—a direct strike, ground current, and the blast effect, to name a few. Because of the myriad ways victims can be injured (cardiac arrest, burns, respiratory arrest, neurological injury, and other trauma), you should initiate the ABCs as soon as the scene is secure. Evacuate as necessary.

Rock Slides

Problem: Rock slides occur quite often in the canyon and have the potential to be deadly. Due to the amount of loose rock along cliffs and in drainages, the canyon is ripe for this type of accident.

Prevention: Do not stand or rest in obvious slide areas. Stay on the trail and do not shortcut the switchbacks. This action can cause rock slides to rain down on those below you. Listen for rock slides, particularly after severe storms. I've seen one rock slide during my canyon hikes, and it sounded like a far-off jet plane at first, then turned into the classic rock-tumbling noise I remembered from movies.

Treatment: As in many of these scenarios, the injuries will vary, so treat the victim accordingly, initiate the ABCs, and evacuate as needed.

Snake and Insect Bites

Problem: The Grand Canyon does harbor a few poisonous critters. The ones you should be most wary of are black widow and brown recluse spiders, scorpions, and rattlesnakes. While these are some of the most venomous creatures in the country, you'll find that they usually avoid humans. It's only by being careless that you risk injury.

Prevention: Don't handle any of these critters. I have read that in Tucson, AZ, at least one person each year is rushed to the hospital when he (the victim is usually male, young, and often under the influence) is struck by a rattlesnake as he tries to kiss it—NOT SMART. Don't stick your hands or feet into or under anything where you can't see—bushes, brush, dark corners, etcetera. Leave your tent zipped up tight, and check your boots and any clothing left outside your

Ancient ruins near the Kaibab Bridge.

A nice rest spot near Tapeats Narrows, Bright Angel Trail.

tent before putting them on. At night (critters' preferred time for moving about), wear shoes and use a flashlight while you are up and around.

For identification purposes, a female black widow is jet black with a red hourglass on her abdomen. (Males appear lighter and smaller.) A brown recluse is usually reddish to light brown, with inch-long thin legs and a violin shape on the top of its body, with the head of the violin pointing towards the tail of the spider. A scorpion is colored between light brown and straw yellow, about an inch to three inches long, with pincers in front and a long tail, usually curled at the end. That tip holds its stinger.

A rattlesnake is a snake with rattles—stay away from it. I've never seen a rattlesnake while hiking the canyon, but care must always be taken to avoid a strike. In some cases, you will hear the rattle long before you can see the snake. If you hear the buzz of a rattler, freeze immediately and (without moving your head if possible) locate the snake with your gaze. Once the snake relaxes from a striking position, slowly move away. If you are within about three feet of the snake, you are in immediate danger of a strike. Double that distance, and you should be well out of its striking range.

Treatment: Most spider bites are initially painless, with intense pain setting in after 10 to 20 minutes. Although patients may think they are dying, only a few people in the United States die from spider bites each year, though thousands are bitten. Common symptoms are weakness, cramping, fever, chills, and nausea. General treatment is to wash the site and apply an antiseptic and a cold compress, administer pain killers, and evacuate.

On the other hand, a scorpion's sting hurts right away and can feel like a bad bee sting or worse. Death usually only occurs from severe allergic reaction in children or the elderly. I've been stung six different times by scorpions, and it's never been a big deal, although for others the pain can be severe. Cooling the sting site is the best treatment, but if the victim has difficulty swallowing, heavy sweating, blurred vision, or other such troublesome signs, have him or her evacuated immediately.

When suffering from snakebite, quickly move away from the snake and stay calm. The area of the bite may swell dramatically, so remove any tight clothing or jewelry. While nearly a third of snake bites are nonvenomous, "dry" bites, you should still use a Sawyer Extractor within about three minutes and keep it applied for about thirty minutes. Do not apply cold, do not administer pain killers, do not give alcohol to the victim, and don't use a tourniquet. Immobilize and splint the wound, then evacuate.

Water Intoxication (AKA hyponatremia)

Problem: In talking with a park ranger at Phantom Ranch, I was told that hyponatremia is the most common problem he saw canyon hikers suffer from. This is another heat-related illness that can happen when you drink a lot of water without eating anything. I have to admit that I'm one of those people who tend to eat less when I'm on the trail. This can cause an imbalance of electrolytes so severe that you could end up suffering a seizure, a coma, or even death. Although this condition is really the opposite of dehydration, the symptoms are nearly identical: disorientation, nausea, vomiting, and fatigue.

Prevention: Don't drink just water alone; mix in some electrolyte-containing sport drinks. You'll also need to eat more than your normal intake of food (especially high-sodium foods) while hiking the canyon to help in avoiding hyponatremia.

Treatment: Rest and eat salty foods. If symptoms progress, protect the victim during possible seizures and monitor breathing. Even if you recognize the symptoms and treat this condition right away, the victim may need to be evacuated.

Side Step: Photography

I have to admit that I'm still "old school" concerning photography. I usually carry about three pounds of Nikon F-100 SLR (Single Lens Reflex) with a 24-120 wide-zoom lens. I shoot mostly slow speed, high color saturation, negative print film (and I bring a handful, plus batteries and a few other filters). I have purchased a little 5 megapixel digital camera that fits in my pocket, and I use it for a lot of the more documentary photos. I still use the old SLR or a medium format camera when trying to capture the grand landscapes.

Digital cameras are great. They are usually light, they allow for easy manipulation with a computer, and they can hold a lot of photos on a small memory card in lieu of carrying lots of film. The quest for cost-effective 8 megapixel cameras (with a resolution comparable to that of 35mm SLRs) is now being met by the camera manufacturers. One disadvantage digital cameras have is that when shooting into the sun and some other elements of the sky, the photo can show "banding" in lieu of smooth transitions.

Other basic tips include using a wide-angle setting for landscapes, while portraits can be enhanced by using the telephoto setting and getting close up. Shoot in the early morning and later afternoon for the best light conditions. At midday most landscapes are subject to flat light and a lack of contrast, but always try to avoid high contrasts of light and dark areas of the photo. Also, when shooting wide-angle landscapes, try to have some interesting focal point in the foreground too (such as an old twisted juniper, flowers, or a colorful shrub).

In the canyon each season has its own attributes for producing wonderful photographs. In late spring the cacti come into bloom. (This is my favorite time for photography.) In winter there can be snow on the rim, while in the summer wildflowers such as penstemon, Indian paintbrush, and desert marigolds bloom. Flowers can be prolific after spring rains. In late fall rabbitbrush turns yellow, and many other plants are enhanced with an autumn hue.

Chapter Six

Geology and the Canyon Colors

Walk on a
rainbow trail;
Walk on a trail
of song,
And all about you
will be beauty.

Navajo song

Grand Canyon Geology Brief

One mile deep, ten miles across, and over 277 river miles long, the Grand Canyon is one of the most striking land areas in the world. The immensity of it all, the incomparable range of colors, and the variety of stunning landforms, leaves visitors in awe the first time they lay eyes on its miraculous composition. Almost immediately, the canyon begs the question, "How was it formed?"

In a nutshell: Ancient seas have repeatedly covered and then withdrawn from vast areas of the American Southwest. Layers of sediments were deposited during the recurring influx of oceans and ultimately solidified into horizontal strata. Modern geologists believe that subsequent natural forces began lifting the huge landmass known as the Colorado Plateau, while the Colorado River later began to erode and etch into the land. This combination of uplift

Lipan Point along Desert View Drive on the South Rim.

and erosion from the river and all its many drainage areas, often along natural fault lines, is what has exposed the stunning multicolored horizontal layering visible today.

The canyon cuts precipitously through a dry, hot plateau that lies between 5,000 and 9,000 feet above sea level. This region of the Southwest has few perennial water sources, yet it is sharply eroded, exposing such varied formations as lava flows, buttes, sheer cliff walls, and intrusions of igneous rock. The plateau maintains a general downward slope from northeast to southwest, with a heavily forested North Rim, and a South Rim more sparsely covered with smaller varieties of piñon and juniper. The vegetation of the inner canyon consists mostly of prickly pear and other cactus varieties, agave, yucca, Mormon tea, and saltbush, with taller cottonwood, redbud, and willow trees growing only where there is ample water. Interestingly, many of the cottonwood trees encountered on these trails were actually planted around the turn of the 20th century. There is very little actual soil in the Grand Canyon, the healthiest being a nitrogen-building black crust called cryptobiotic soil. (One should avoid disturbing this essential building block of the desert.)

The top layers of the canyon were formed about 270 million years ago, while at the bottom of the canyon, the oldest rocks are estimated to be nearly 2 billion years old. While winds abrade the rock surface to some degree, erosion is mainly the work of the rains, loosening grains of sand and flowing, sometimes as massive walls of debris, through the variety of washes, arroyos, and canyons, scouring everything in the path. These floods and debris flows cut into canyon walls, undermining the harder layers above. Without adequate support, gravity prevails and cliff walls collapse. The powerful Colorado River ultimately carries this material toward the Gulf of California in a cycle that has been ongoing for thousands of millennia.

Many books cover the full geological history of the Grand Canyon. For our purposes, I have provided trail profiles on page 87, including the rock formations estimated to be occurring at the different elevations of each trail. These profiles are provided more for general information than for a textbook examination of the geology found in the Grand Canyon. Please note that these profiles are the author's best guess-timations and are not to scale.

Sunrise at Point Imperial with Mount Hayden on the right, North Rim.

 ## Side Step: Native Americans Indigenous to the Region

Although paleo-hunters were present in the Southwest some 10,000 years ago, there is little evidence of their culture. The first known inhabitants of the canyon were hunter-gatherers, evidenced to have been active in the region around 2000 B.C., but for reasons unknown these people subsequently left the canyon 1,000 years later (although many archeologists believe they didn't actually leave but became more nomadic). The Basketmakers (Ancestral Puebloans) settled the canyon about A.D. 500. They lived in a more communal society, growing irrigated crops, hunting, trading extensively, and eventually building pueblos along and below the rims. Then, around A.D. 1200, the Puebloans abandoned the area, when (as some speculate) the Southwest experienced a prolonged drought. The Hopi are their descendants, now residing near the center of the Navajo Reservation in Arizona.

By the 1300s, the Hualapai and Havasupai settled along the South Rim (and still own lands to the west of the National Park along the Colorado River). The Paiutes moved south from what is now Utah to the canyon's North Rim. The Navajo (Diné) migrated from the Northwest beginning in the 1400s. The Navajo thrived in the area and are today the United State's largest Native American tribe, their reservation encompassing a large part of northeastern Arizona.

Grand Canyon National Park General Information

Mail: Grand Canyon National Park
PO Box 129
Grand Canyon, AZ 86023
Phone: (928) 638-7888
To report an overdue hiker:
(928) 638-7888
Web: www.nps.gov/grca/

Grand Canyon Backcountry Office

Mail: Backcountry Information Center
Grand Canyon National Park
PO Box 129
Grand Canyon, AZ 86023
Phone: (928) 638-7875 (Monday -
Friday from 1 to 5 p.m.)
Fax: (928) 638-2125
Web: www.nps.gov/grca/planyourvisit/
backcounty.htm

South Rim Campgrounds

**Mather Campground
(National Park Service):**
Phone: (800) 365-2267
Web: http://reservations.nps.gov/

Desert View Campground (NPS):
First come, first served—see information, page 16.

**Ten-X Campground
or dispersed camping:**
Mail: Tusayan Ranger District
Kaibab National Forest
PO Box 3088
Grand Canyon, AZ 86023
Phone: (928) 638-2443

North Rim Campgrounds

**North Rim Campground
(National Park Service):**
Phone: (800) 365-2267
Web: http://reservations.nps.gov/

**De Motte Campground,
Jacob Lake Campground,
and dispersed camping:**
Call Kaibab Plateau Visitor Center
at Jacob Lake
Phone: (928) 643-7298 or...

Mail: North Kaibab Ranger District
Kaibab National Forest
PO Box 248
Fredonia, AZ 86022
Phone: (928) 643-7395
Web: www.fs.fed.us/r3/kai/recreation

Kaibab Camper Village:
Phone: (928) 643-7804
Or: (800) 525-0924
Web: www.kaibabcampervillage.com

South Rim Lodging

For information and reservations at Phantom Ranch (Inner Canyon), El Tovar, Bright Angel Lodge and Cabins, Yavapai Lodge, Maswik Lodge, or Trailer Village contact:

Mail: Xanterra Central Reservations
Xanterra Parks and Resorts
6312 S. Fiddlers Green, #600N
Greenwood Village, CO 80111
Web: www.xanterra.com

Or: Xanterra Parks and Resorts
    PO Box 699
    Grand Canyon, AZ 86023
Phone: (888) 297-2757
Or: (928) 638-2631 (guest contact
    or same-day reservations)
Bright Angel Travel Desk:
    (928) 638-3283
Web: www.grandcanyonlodges.com

North Rim Lodging

Grand Canyon Lodge:
(See above contact information for
    Xanterra Parks and Resorts)
Web: www.grandcanyonnorthrim.com

Kaibab Lodge:
Phone: (928) 638-2389
Web: www.kaibablodge.com

Jacob Lake Inn:
Phone: (928) 643-7232
Web: www.jacoblake.com

Other Contacts

Havasupai and Havasu Falls:
Mail: Havasupai Tourist Enterprises
    PO Box 160
    Supai, AZ 86435
Phone: (928) 448-2121 or 448-2141
Web: www.havasupaitribe.com

Rim to Rim Shuttle:
Mail: Trans-Canyon Shuttle:
    PO Box 348
    Grand Canyon, AZ 86023
Phone: (928) 638-2820
Schedule: Departs N. Rim: 7 a.m.
    Arrives S. Rim: 12 p.m.
    Departs S. Rim: 1:30 p.m.
    Arrives N. Rim: 6:30 p.m.

South Rim Kennel:
Open: Daily from 7:30 a.m. to 5:00 p.m.
Phone: (928) 638-0534

Maps and Books:
Grand Canyon Association
Phone: (928) 638-2481
Or: (800) 858-2808, ext 7030
Web: www.grandcanyon.org

Wilderness Medicine (First-Aid) and
Backpacking Training:
National Outdoor Leadership School
Phone: (800) 710-6657
Web: www.nols.edu

Weather Updates:
Web: www.noaa.gov
Or: www.nps.gov/archive/grca/grand-
canyon/weather.htm

Radio Information: KSGC-FM 92.1
Or: (928) 638-9552

Early November snowfall as seen from the Rim Trail, South Rim.

Backcountry Permit Request Form
Grand Canyon National Park

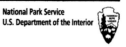

Submit form by Fax (928-638-2125) or mail (Backcountry Information Center, Grand Canyon National Park, PO Box 129, Grand Canyon, AZ 86023).

Name _____

Address _____

Address _____

City _____

State _____ Zip _____

Country _____

Home Phone _____

Work Phone _____

# of people _____ # of stock _____

Trailhead Vehicle 1 (State/Lic. Plate) _____

Trailhead Vehicle 2 (State/Lic. Plate) _____

Organization _____

Note: If this is part of a larger group obtaining more than one permit, you must enter an Organization name. Because of the potential damages caused by social trailing, regulations stipulate that all permits are void when a group obtains multiple permits for the same campground or use area for the same night. The alternative for these "larger groups" is to obtain permits for smaller groups and ensure the itineraries for these permits never bring more than one of the permits into the same campground or use area on the same night. If your permit is for 6 or less people, please keep gatherings to a maximum of 6 and select areas where impact to the canyon will be minimized. Please include the name of your "larger group" as your "Organization" name.

First Choice:

Date	Use Area or Campsite
1. _____	_____
2. _____	_____
3. _____	_____
4. _____	_____
5. _____	_____
6. _____	_____

(itinerary requests can be longer than 6 nights)

Second Choice:

Date	Use Area or Campsite
1. _____	_____
2. _____	_____
3. _____	_____
4. _____	_____
5. _____	_____
6. _____	_____

Third Choice: (attach additional choices as needed)

Date	Use Area or Campsite
1. _____	_____
2. _____	_____
3. _____	_____
4. _____	_____
5. _____	_____
6. _____	_____

Willing to accept variations to:

[ ] Start Date between _____ and _____

[ ] Campsites

[ ] Trip length - *this will affect cost*

　　minimum nights:___, maximum nights:____

Option for those requesting large group space:

[ ] If space for a large group (7-11 people) is not available, I will accept a permit for 6 people.

Frequent Hiker Membership Program (Costs $25 for a year and waives the $10 permit fee for 12 months. Members are still responsible for the $5 per person per night charge and for park entrance fees upon arrival.)

[ ] I am already a member   [ ] Please enroll me for 1 year for $25   [ ] No thanks

Payment Information: (Pay by Credit Card or Check. Denied requests will not incur a charge. **Payments are non-refundable.**)

Credit Card Number: ☐☐☐☐ - ☐☐☐☐ - ☐☐☐☐ - ☐☐☐☐   Exp. Date: ☐☐ / ☐☐

Total Authorized Permit Cost $_____ ($10 fee plus $5 per person per night, all non-refundable)

Cardholder Name _____ Authorizing Signature _____

Rev. Apr/02

Trait Profiles

Bright Angel Trail

* = seasonal water

- Trailhead (6,850')
- Mile-and-a-Half Resthouse (5,700')
- Three-Mile Resthouse (4,700')
- Indian Garden (3,800')
- The Devil's Corkscrew (3,200')
- River Resthouse (2,500')
- Confluence- Colorado River & Bright Angel Creek (2,450')
- Bright Angel Bridge (2,500')
- Bright Angel Campground (2,450')
- Phantom Ranch (2,550')

Mileage: 1 mile 2 miles 3 miles 4 miles 5 miles 6 miles 7 miles 8 miles 9 miles

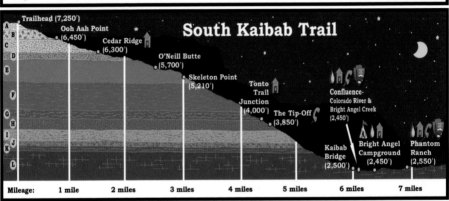

South Kaibab Trail

- Trailhead (7,250')
- Ooh Aah Point (6,450')
- Cedar Ridge (6,300')
- O'Neill Butte (5,700')
- Skeleton Point (5,210')
- Tonto Trail Junction (4,000')
- The Tip-Off (3,850')
- Confluence- Colorado River & Bright Angel Creek (2,450')
- Kaibab Bridge (2,500')
- Bright Angel Campground (2,450')
- Phantom Ranch (2,550')

Mileage: 1 mile 2 miles 3 miles 4 miles 5 miles 6 miles 7 miles

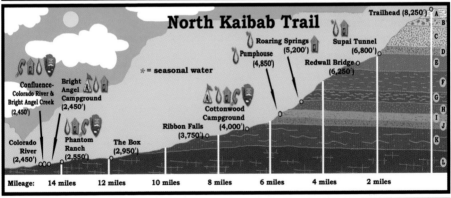

North Kaibab Trail

Trailhead (8,250')

* = seasonal water

- Supai Tunnel (6,800')
- Roaring Springs (5,200')
- Redwall Bridge (6,250')
- Pumphouse (4,850')
- Cottonwood Campground (4,000')
- Ribbon Falls (3,750')
- The Box (2,950')
- Phantom Ranch (2,550')
- Bright Angel Campground (2,450')
- Confluence- Colorado River & Bright Angel Creek (2,450')
- Colorado River (2,450')

Mileage: 14 miles 12 miles 10 miles 8 miles 6 miles 4 miles 2 miles

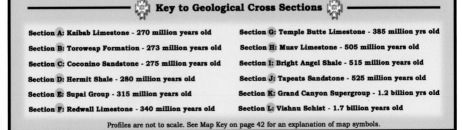

Key to Geological Cross Sections

Section A: Kaibab Limestone - 270 million years old

Section B: Toroweap Formation - 273 million years old

Section C: Coconino Sandstone - 275 million years old

Section D: Hermit Shale - 280 million years old

Section E: Supai Group - 315 million years old

Section F: Redwall Limestone - 340 million years old

Section G: Temple Butte Limestone - 385 million yrs old

Section H: Muav Limestone - 505 million years old

Section I: Bright Angel Shale - 515 million years old

Section J: Tapeats Sandstone - 525 million years old

Section K: Grand Canyon Supergroup - 1.2 billion yrs old

Section L: Vishnu Schist - 1.7 billion years old

Profiles are not to scale. See Map Key on page 42 for an explanation of map symbols.

"Even to remember that the Grand Canyon is still there lifts up the heart."

J.B. Priestly